HIGHER EDUCATION
for the FUTURE

Charles Carter

BASIL BLACKWELL · OXFORD

First published 1980 by
Basil Blackwell Publisher
5 Alfred Street
Oxford OX1 4HB
England

British Library Cataloguing in Publication Data

Carter, Sir Charles Frederick
    A higher education for the future. –
    (Mainstream series).
    1.   Education, Higher – Great Britain – 1965 –
    I. Title II. Series
    378.41   LA637

ISBN 0–631–11331–2

Typeset by Cotswold Typesetting Gloucester Ltd. and
Printed in Great Britain by Billing & Sons Ltd.
Guildford, London, Oxford and Worcester.

CONTENTS

PROLOGUE

It is not easy to give an exact definition of higher education. In Britain, education in school is compulsory up to the age of 16: so we can distinguish all education beyond 16 as 'post-compulsory education'. Some of this is provided for children who stay on at school after 16, commonly to the age of 18 (to take a 'sixth form course'); some is provided in further education colleges, but is equivalent to what might otherwise have been obtained in the sixth form of a school; some is to be found in further education colleges or the training establishments of employers, and not in the schools, but is considered as having a level or intellectual content no greater than sixth form work. (Note the appearance of the assumption that 'level' is a clearly ascertainable measurement, which it certainly is not.) Then there is the great range of courses provided for adults, either to extend cultural or leisure interests or to give additional training for work. At one extreme, no one would consider a twelve-session course in lampshade-making for bored suburban house-wives to be 'higher education': at the other, an advanced course in engineering production methods, intended for engineering graduates or other Chartered Engineers, would plainly be 'higher education', though it would not necessarily take place in an *institution* of higher education.

The common practice (which I follow in this book) is to define higher education as that part of post-compulsory education which builds on, and goes beyond, sixth form studies in the schools or their equivalent taken elsewhere. It will thus include adult or 'continuing' education which requires this background. All the rest may be called 'further education', though some ambiguity will still remain in the classification of 'adult education'. The definition will do well enough, provided one remembers that the content and nature of sixth form studies is changing – with the effect, as some believe, that work previously done in the schools is being shifted into higher education: and also that problems will remain in defining the 'level' of educational opportunities provided, not for 18-year-olds, but later in life.

Some people would wish to narrow the definition further by referring to education as 'higher' if it goes beyond the requirements of the Advanced level of the General Certificate of Education. But this will not do, in discussing what is to happen in the future: the 'A-level' may itself have disappeared in another twenty years, being replaced by examinations of different content. Sixth forms will increasingly include students who would not appropriately attempt A-level examinations, nor go on to full degree studies; but there is no reliable measurement which enables us to distinguish potential graduates, and it will be more fruitful to define 'higher education' so that we can also look at less demanding courses beyond the sixth form.

It would be easier, of course, if we could say that higher education is the activity of particular institutions. This appears to be what the Carnegie Commission and Council in the United States have assumed: I have not been able to trace, in their numerous reports, any other clear definition of field. A recent report lists 2837 universities and colleges in the U.S. which are held to provide higher education, the line of demarcation being set by 'accreditation', which in general is a requirement for eligibility for federal and state student aid. But this approach will not do for Britain. We still have significant amounts of professional study, at a level equivalent to other higher education, which lies outside the universities and colleges; and we have a significant number of colleges which exist mainly for 'further' education, but include some higher education courses. An institutional definition would thus bring in much lower level work, while omitting some which is at professional degree level.

The distinction between a definition in terms of persons and one in terms of institutions is important in discussing purposes. Thus, the Carnegie Commission report on 'The Purposes and the Performance of Higher Education in the United States' (June 1973) lists some purposes which belong to the educational process as applied to individuals:

The provision of opportunities for the intellectual, aesthetic, ethical, and skill development of individual students. The advancement of human capability in society at large. The enlargement of educational justice for the postsecondary age group.

and others which arise from organized activity in the institutions:

The provision of campus environments which can constructively assist students in their more general developmental growth. The transmission and advancement of learning and wisdom. The critical evaluation of society – through individual thought and persuasion – for the sake of society's self-renewal.

The same distinction runs through this book. It begins by looking at the future of higher education as a provider of educated or trained people, and as a means of enlargement of individual opportunity. Then it turns to the institutions and their organisation, remembering that research, scholarship and general public service are seen as part of their function as well as the teaching of individuals.

It may seem tiresome to begin with definitions; but one problem which bedevils the discussion of higher education, particularly if it includes any international comparisons, is the uncertainty of the use of words. The words translated as 'university', 'college', 'degree', and many others, do not mean exactly the same thing in different countries, and it is sometimes uncertain what they mean in a British context. So the reader must excuse me if I sometimes try to make clear what I am writing about.

1

WHAT EXISTS NOW

British higher education is both complex and changing, and describing it is not made easier by the fact that the statisticians of the education departments frustrate the excellence of their coverage by a delay in publication so long that it is difficult to use their results. The starting point is the definition of higher education given in the Prologue, which can be rephrased to say that higher education includes only those courses which lie beyond the Advanced level of the General Certificate of education, or beyond the Ordinary National Certificate (a further education qualification), or their equivalent. The significance of the word 'beyond' is that entrants to the courses would normally have this level of preparation: it does not imply that they *must* have specific prior qualifications at this level, though there are many courses for which this would be true. Looking back a few years, 'higher education' was also deemed to include teacher training, even though entry to a course for a teacher's Certificate could at that time be obtained without sixth form study. This anomaly has, however, disappeared with a change in the professional requirements for teachers.

It is not necessary to go to a university or college in order to obtain higher education. Significant numbers of people, though exactly how many cannot readily be discovered, study for professional qualifications on their own, or use the help of correspondence courses and private tutors. Most students, however, will seek an attachment to an 'institution' of higher education – a term which is used often in this book, because much of the discussion in it does not relate to universities alone, or to further education colleges alone, but to all or to a cross-section of the whole complex of 'institutions'. (They are

1

alternatively referred to as 'universities and colleges'). That complex includes:

> *The universities, which are independent corporate bodies.*
> *The polytechnics, which are owned or assisted by local authorities.*
> *Other colleges doing 'advanced work', that is, higher education.*
> *(In Scotland there are 'central institutions' which do broadly the same sort of work as polytechnics, or departments in them, but are financed directly by central government. In Northern Ireland the polytechnic is also financed by central government.)*

Most of the 'other colleges' are further education colleges, owned by local authorities, and (for the most part) primarily concerned with non-advanced work. This group also includes the English 'direct grant institutions' which are funded by the Department of Education and Science. Two of these, the Royal College of Art and Cranfield Institute of Technology, are of 'university status' in the sense that they confer degrees. The rest are typically specialist institutions for agriculture, nursing or seamanship.

The pattern becomes more complex when we bring in the teacher training colleges. Until recently, teacher training outside the universities was the business of a large number of colleges, generally doing nothing other than teacher training. Most of these belonged to local authorities (though in Scotland and Northern Ireland they were directly financed by central government), but there were also 'voluntary' colleges associated with the churches or otherwise having independent charitable status, and these received direct grants from central government for capital purposes, their current costs being met by local authorities. In the reorganization of teacher training which followed a reappraisal of training needs in 1972, it was decided to reduce the number of colleges (and break down the 'monotechnic' system) by closures and amalgamations. A few colleges have amalgamated with universities, and some with polytechnics. Others have joined with further education colleges; others again have remained without amalgamation, and are described as 'free-standing', but have enlarged the range of their courses, typically describing themselves as 'Colleges of Higher Education'. Finally, in a few special cases, colleges have continued as separate specialist teacher training institutions.

This process of change is not yet complete, and it is inadequately reflected in the statistics. However, the Oakes report on the Management of Higher Education in the Maintained Sector (see p. 42) contains a table showing the expectation (in 1978) of the position in 1981 in England and Wales. Adding the university sector, this shows:

Universities (including postgraduate business schools, but not the Open University)	37	
(Note: the colleges of the Universities of London and of Wales are not counted separately)		68
The Open University	1	
Polytechnics	30	
Institutions with more than ninety per cent advanced work:		
Former Colleges of Education, freestanding or amalgamated	57	
Colleges of Music, Drama, Art, Design	5	67
Other F.E. (Further Education) Colleges (including two Direct Grant)	5	

Institutions with thirty to ninety
  per cent advanced work:

Former Colleges of Education, now amalgamated	18	
Colleges of Music, Drama, Art, Design, Agriculture	24	} 57
Other F.E. Colleges (including one Direct Grant)	15	

Institutions with less than thirty
  per cent advanced work:

Former Colleges of Education, now amalgamated	2	
Colleges of Art, Design, Agriculture	7	} 264
Other F.E. Colleges	255	

456

A similar table for Scotland would show eight universities, fourteen 'central institutions', ten colleges of education, and some 200 other institutions with a share of advanced work. Northern Ireland has two universities, a polytechic and three teachers' colleges: some advanced work also exists in four other institutions.

The institutions other than the universities are described as the 'public sector' of higher education; within the public sector, the 'maintained sector' consists of those colleges which are financed by local education authorities. The whole system is often described as 'binary', that is, divided between the universities and the public sector. Indeed, in one sense it has been so divided for very many years, and there was no new departure of government policy to make it so, though there was for a period a definite policy to increase the proportion of the public sector in the whole. But in a more significant sense the system has three parts: the universities; the public sector institutions which are primarily concerned with advanced work, such as the polytechnics and the colleges of higher education; and the public sector institutions in which advanced work is a minor accompaniment of less advanced studies. It would be convenient to be able to forget about the last group, especially as the weight of government policy has been to concentrate advanced work in fewer institutions. However, although there are many colleges in which advanced work is the concern of a small minority, the multiplicity of these colleges means that their total advanced student numbers are by no means insignificant. Higher education courses can be divided into three groups: those leading to first and higher degrees; those leading to Higher National Diplomas (for full-time study) or to Higher National Certificates (for part-time study), these being further education qualifications which are nationally validated; and the rest, typically courses of study for professional qualifications. The table derived from the Oakes Committee report, shown above, can be extended to show in which groups there are more than 5000 students in a particular class of establishment:

	DEGREES	HND/HNC	OTHER
Universities	X		(1)
Polytechnics	X	X	X
Former Colleges of Education:			
over ninety per cent advanced work	X		(2)
thirty to ninety per cent advanced work	X	X	(2)
Other F.E. Colleges:			
thirty to ninety per cent advanced work		X	X
under thirty per cent advanced work		X	X

(1) Professional studies in universities are generally associated with degree work.

(2) The Oakes report shows considerable numbers under these heads (for 1975/6), but most will have been Certificate of Education students who in future will take degrees.

The broad picture of 'who does what' is thus that universities, polytechnics, and former colleges of education provide degrees; polytechnics and other further education colleges, including some amalgamated colleges of education, offer the Higher National Diploma and the Higher National Certificate; and the polytechnics and further education colleges do courses for professional qualifications which are not associated with degrees. An analogous division exists in Scotland and Northern Ireland.

Looking in more detail at what goes on in higher education institutions, we can distinguish:

Courses for first degrees (which in most places would be termed Bachelors' degrees, though in Scotland the first degree may be a Master's degree, and at Oxford and Cambridge a lapse of time and the payment of a modest fee will upgrade a Bachelor's to a Master's degree).

Courses for higher degrees (that is, Masters' or Doctors' degrees, the courses or research for which assume knowledge equivalent to the possession of a first degree, though the actual award of a first degree is not always a necessary condition).

Courses for diplomas and certificates: in addition to the HND and HNC, institutions freely invent their own diplomas and certificates as marks of achievement below first degree level, or intermediate betweeen a first and a higher degree.

Courses for recognized professional qualifications, such as those of doctors, accountants, architects, surveyors or engineers.

Courses not leading to any specific qualification or award: for instance, the increasingly important short 'refresher courses' which people take in order to extend and up-date their knowledge.

This teaching work is sometimes associated with activities

of research or public service which are further discussed in Chapter 8.

Diplomas and certificates are an unregulated market, and, where such qualifications have been instituted by universities or colleges, it is not possible to be sure to what level of work they relate. The HND and the HNC, however, are controlled nationally by the Business and Technician Education Councils (with separate arrangements for Scotland) so that variations in particular colleges can be made to relate to a common level of achievement. Degrees and (most) professional qualifications are regulated, and there is much less variation of standard than exists in some other countries. The right to give degrees belongs to each university, and is set out in its constitution. Some universities have explicit power to grant degrees 'externally', that is, to students who are not, in the normal sense, members of the university and who are taught elsewhere, in Britain or abroad. The University of London had a large, though now reduced, business in external degrees in many other institutions. The most important other use of the power to give external degrees is now the 'validation' by universities of degrees taken in some of the former colleges of education, including degrees in subjects other than 'education' (that is, preparation for school-teaching). Degrees are also given by the Council for National Academic Awards, established in 1964, which exists to provide the opportunity of taking degrees to students in institutions which have no independent power to confer them – such as the polytechnics. The CNAA approves courses and teaching arrangements proposed by the colleges, and thereafter monitors the examining process so as to ensure consistency of standard, not only for all CNAA degrees, but between their degrees and those given by the universities. The universities seek to ensure consistency of standard by the use, in the great majority of places, of external examiners, mostly drawn from other universities.

In a simple case, a professional qualification is conferred under powers obtained by the corporate bodies of the profession, allowing for the setting of examinations. Thus a barrister is 'called to the Bar' after passing the Bar examinations and fulfilling other conditions, such as the consumption of a certain number of dinners at his Inn of Court. Most professions now find, however, that it is necessary to recognize examinations taken for other educational qualifications as giving partial (or, in some instances, complete) exemption from their own examinations. Thus an accountant can reduce the number of examinations to be taken, and shorten his period of training, if he has previously taken a degree; and parts of the profession appear to be moving towards a system by which a relevant degree would provide the whole of the theoretical training, and the requirements for professional membership would then be completed by a period of practical experience and by passing a test of professional competence. Degree training followed by practical experience has become the common route for professional engineers. But not all professions regulate themselves: thus, the status of qualified teacher is a recognition by government that the student has been successful in theoretical and practical examinations for teacher training (validated by a university or by CNAA), and that he or she is also certified to be a proper person to enter the teaching profession (that is, free from gross moral disability).

Apart from the Open University, which was of course founded for part-time study, the university undergraduate students are nearly all full-time; but the universities have the great majority of the higher degree students, and many of these are part-time. The former colleges of education are mostly concerned with full-time work, but the polytechnics and the other colleges contain significant numbers of part-time students at all levels of work. Forward estimates for the year 1980–81 (at present being raised downwards) provided for 530,000 full-time students in Great Britain, including 'sandwich course' students – that is, those absent for practical training at intervals during a full-time course – and for 305,000 part-time students (this figure omits those in universities other than the Open Univeristy). Of the full-time students, 301,000 were expected to be in universities and 229,000 elsewhere; of the part-time students, 131.000 were expected to be in the Open University and

174,000 elsewhere. There are over three and a half million further and adult education students at levels below higher education.

The universities have a monopoly of degree-level teaching of some subjects, such as agriculture, medicine, dentistry and veterinary science. They are also the principal home of degree-level teaching in the humanities, and are much stronger than the polytechnics and the other colleges in science. The strength of the public-sector colleges lies in social, administrative and business studies, in professional subjects such as architecture, and, at least as a proportion of the student body, in engineering. Although degrees in education are mostly taken in the former colleges of education, the universities provide a major alternative route into the teaching profession through the post-graduate certificate, a course of training which gives qualified teacher status to graduates in other subjects. However – to underline the point that there are few simple statements about British higher education which are true – it should be mentioned that some of the colleges of education also provide courses for a post-graduate certificate.

What, then, is the difference between a university and a polytechnic or other college? Although they tend to teach a different mixture of subjects, and a different mixture of levels of course, these characteristics will provide no definite dividing line. The university sector gets its money by a different route, but in this respect is not fundamentally different from the direct grant institutions. The universities have a far greater commitment to research, but the polytechnics are not at all pleased to be regarded as purely concerned with teaching. The universities do nothing significant except for higher education and research, and at one time it was asserted that they could thus be distinguished from institutions which had a (supposedly beneficial) spread of advanced and non-advanced work. However, the non-university sector now contains many institutions which have virtually none of the lower level work. Efforts have been made to portray the public sector colleges as 'more socially responsive': but this will not do either, for the universities' record in experiment to meet new social and economic needs is very good. One suspects that those who used phrases about 'social responsiveness' really meant that the public sector colleges are more capable of being ordered about. The only valid definition of the difference relates to the constitution or legal status of the institution. A university in Britain is a private corporate body, not part of any department of state nor answerable to any minister or local government body; hence it is not in the 'public sector', even though it is critically dependent on money given by government. In most cases it exercises its functions because of the grant by the Crown of a Royal Charter, which establishes it in perpetuity (unless some later King or Queen should revoke the Charter), defines what it can do, and indicates what officers and governing bodies it will have. The Charter gives power to make statutes, which are 'laws' defining in more detail how the university should operate, and these have to be approved by the Privy Council, which in theory is a private body of advisers to the Crown. With some exceptions, for example in Scotland, Parliament has had nothing to do with the constitution of the universities or with their subsequent control; they remain totally free to do anything permitted by their Charters, and in any way.

In contrast, the institutions owned by local authorities (the 'maintained' sector) are run by governing bodies appointed by those authorities, and thus responsible and answerable to a democratically elected council. It is usual to give governing bodies, especially of polytechnics, a fair amount of freedom, but this is limited by the desire for consistency across the local authority's services: thus a request from a director of a polytechnic to appoint an extra secretary may be refused because it would give rise to awkward comparisons. A university's establishment of posts is decided by itself, and is constrained only by its total budget. In the local authority institutions, detailed budgetary control is exercised, and control may extend to the approval of purchases and the regulation of staff conditions. The local authority is also responsible for ensuring that the provision made is related to regional planning decisions taken by the Regional Advisory Councils for Further Education (or their successors under any national Advanced Further Education Councils): this means that the maintained institution does not have, as a university does, an absolute right to establish a new course on its own initiative and without delay, but may have first to consult the Regional Advisory Council and HM Inspectors. Further delay may be caused by the need to get approval from the Council for National Academic Awards. The controls on the direct grant and voluntary colleges are differently operated, and are less onerous on the administrative side; where they have their own diplomas, certificates or degrees they have more academic freedom, but otherwise they will be subject to much the same limits as apply in the maintained sector.

The total sum of money to be provided for the universities is set by government after a dialogue with the University Grants Committee, which is largely composed of university professors (this lump being leavened by a few industrialists and other outside members). The Committee has a full-time chairman and a substantial secretariat, and they inevitably have a major influence on the part-time committee members. The UGC is responsible for dividing the global sum between universities. The method at present used determines for each university each year a total current income from grant and student fees, so that – apart from endowment income, which is very substantial at Oxford and Cambridge but negligible at many newer universities – the UGC fixes what the university can spend, unless it can draw on balances from earlier years. There are normally forecasts of grant for later years, but these, in the absence of any assurance about how changing prices will be allowed for, are not of much use for planning purposes. Grants for buildings are specific, and the UGC exercises a detailed control of building plans and standards; grants for equipment and furniture can be used only for those purposes, but are not controlled in detail apart from a few large items; and the general 'recurrent grant' can be used in any way, for virtually any purpose proper to the functions of the university.

In contrast, there is no precise provision for the public sector colleges. Total local authority income is composed mainly of the produce of the rates, which the authorities can determine for themselves, and the Rate Support Grant, which is determined by central government. At a given level of Rate Support Grant, the incentive for economy is provided by the desire not to ask electors to pay more rates; but, in relation to advanced further education, this incentive is fatally weakened by the operation of a pooling system, spreading expenditure across all authorities, including some who have little provision of higher education of their own. Thus local extravagance is not locally paid for, and, despite efforts at control and advice by government, there is some evidence of lack of financial restraint; the polytechnics, for instance, are – considering their limited commitment to research – remarkably expensive institutions. This is no doubt why it has recently been proposed that a minor share of expenditure should be met, not by the pool, but by the maintaining authority. However, once a budget has been set, it generally provides a closer control than is placed on the universities. Expenditure may be authorised under many different heads, and a formal procedure may be required to obtain permission to transfer money from one head to another.

The public sector and the university sector provide, in fact, an interesting opportunity to contrast a planned and regulated system with one which is allowed great freedom. The public sector colleges are subject to more detailed control both of finance and operation and of academic plans. It is sometimes believed – and perhaps deliberately allowed to be believed – that the UGC controls the academic planning of the universities by issuing directions. But this is almost wholly untrue: there is only one area in which the UGC has a decisive voice, namely that of developments which require new building which cannot be carried out from private funds. It is true that the UGC offers occasional advice to universities, that it 'cannot encourage' new departments of languages, or 'hopes that universities will seriously consider' a larger provision for computer science. It also, in distributing grant, will tell a university that 'provision has not been included' for some item in the estimates; but this is, in most cases, a meaningless remark, since the grant allocation is not built up by adding departmental estimates, but rather by amending a global formula-based allocation to take account of special circumstances. There is little willingness in universities to believe that the UGC knows best, and there are many cases in which advice, thought to be misguided, is ignored. My experience offers no evidence that the UGC worries about this, or even notices that the diversion has occurred. This suggests that the Committee does not seriously believe in itself as a supreme academic planning authority, outside a few expensive areas like medicine (a subject which no university could start without a large building allocation and an assurance of much bigger recurrent funds). It is possible, however, that there will be some movement towards using the UGC as a directing authority, and there is an indication of this in the attempts of government to limit the acceptance of overseas students.

I return to the issue of planning and freedom in Chapter 4. The evidence so far does not suggest that more external planning and regulation leads to greater economy of resources, nor that it produces a more appropriate provision of courses and other activities. Those who work in the public sector, however, argue that this is because so much of their development is recent, and that comparisons with the more experienced university sector are unfair.

The disposition to discuss British higher education in terms of two or three sectors must not be allowed to obscure the fact that the differences within these sectors are as great as the differences between them. Universities acquire a bias at the period of their foundation which is never wholly removed, whatever further changes occur over the years. Oxford is still recognisably the training-place of members of a ruling class, and its effectiveness may be seen by enquiring where Ministers of the Crown were educated. Leeds, with its strong interest in applied science and medicine, shows the essentially practical concerns of a great industrial city which wanted better provision for its sons and daughters. Salford has the unmistakeable attitudes of a technological university which grew from a technical college, and was transferred from the public to the university sector. The whole group of 'new universities' founded in the 1960s bears the mark of ideas about 'broader' courses which were current at the time, and their date of foundation had the effect of making them less science-based than the older civic and technological institutions.

Similarly polytechnics show differences arising from the different routes by which they have attained that status, from the different policies of their governing bodies, particularly about the continuance of lower level work, and from the varied patterns of amalgamation (for instance, with colleges of education or of art) which have occurred. The former colleges of education, even if they have escaped amalgamation, have followed different paths: for instance, Charlotte Mason College at Ambleside continues as a small 'monotechnic', concentrating on honours degree work and with entrance requirements more severe than some universities, while some of the larger colleges of higher education now have education courses as a minor interest and are mainly concerned with general degrees in the humanities. The 'other further education colleges' include some which could well have aspired to polytechnic status, and which offer a considerable range of advanced work, and others in which a single advanced course persists by some local accident.

Nevertheless, great as is the variety contained in the British system, it is not as varied in the levels of study which it offers as (for instance) higher education in the United States. It is notably short of two-year courses; and it does not adapt itself to the finer divisions of need in society by offering degrees which everyone knows to be of different value. The nation-wide uniformity of the level of attainment expected in a degree is of course something of a fiction, because there are bound to be differences associated with differing average abilities of entrants, and in any case the concept of 'level' is an elusive one when one is comparing courses of very different content. But the differences are neither large enough, nor systematic enough, to produce much effect on the employability of graduates. A large proportion of the total output of the system is therefore competitive for jobs at the same level.

Several advanced countries have a broader system than Britain, providing for a greater proportion of each age group and thus for a greater range of ability. The British system is narrow and selective: the principle in the Robbins report of 1963, that opportunities should exist in higher education for those 'qualified by ability and attainment', left the level of qualification undefined. There is nothing corresponding to a right of entry for all who have reached a certain level in a school leaving examination.

But, within its limited range, the British system is probably more free and more varied than any other which relies predominantly on state finance. The freedom is particularly apparent for the universities. They appoint their own staff without restriction, whereas in a number of European countries staff are employees of the state. They choose their students, and are not bound to take all who offer themselves. They determine what is to be taught and how it is to be taught, constrained only by the overall budget and by certain requirements of professional bodies about the education of their future members. They determine what subjects of research should be pursued, again constrained only by the overall budget. The freedom of the public sector colleges is (as will be seen from the earlier discussion) rather more restricted, but it still compares favourably with most state-run systems, if only because British governments are gentle in dealing with local authorities and allow them much variation of practice.

Higher education in the United States is certainly even more varied, and there is an extension of freedom in having so great a range of opportunities. But those parts which depend on state finance often have to live with a complexity of regulation and a degree of political interference which are not known in Britain. The parts which are privately financed can develop as they may wish, but only if finance is secure. Even great and prestigious private institutions have had their financial troubles, and have had to remember in their policies the necessities of fund-raising. So the freedoms of the American system must not be overstated; indeed, there is much envy in the United States and in other countries for the degree of freedom allowed to British universities, and admiration for the device of the University Grants Committee by which that freedom is made consistent with government financing.

British first degree education appears to be more efficient than that of nearly all other countries, in the sense that the length of course needed to reach a particular level of attainment is shorter. There must be several qualifications to this statement: levels of attainment are not readily compared, a more selective system has a better chance to speed up courses, and the explanation might lie in a better level of preparation in the schools (though this is becoming increasingly implausible). Despite these qualifications, the claim of efficiency probably stands. (The extra costs of a longer course are substantial, for they must include not only the direct expenditure but also the earnings foregone because of a shortening of the student's working life). The British system is also exceptional in the universality and extent of student support for those pursuing first degree courses. Subject to a test of parental means, those accepted for a degree course have a right to a grant for their maintenance, while all who are accepted get their fees paid by the state and the local authorities. A considerable proportion of higher degree work is also state-supported. This universal system should remove any financial difficulty in participation in higher education by students whose parents earn low wages; but in fact the proportion of such students varies little, showing that the obstacles to their entry to higher education must be sought earlier in life, and are not removable by a grant system.

What now exists is reasonably successful, alive and varied. But it will be put to new tests between now and the end of the century, and this book is an attempt to review its purposes and programmes in the light, both of the changes which are to be expected in external circumstance, and of the weaknesses which a careful observer can see to be already present. I turn first to the needs which society seeks to fulfil by having a higher education system.

2

THE NEEDS AND DESIRES
OF SOCIETY

In planning higher education for the future, it is first of all necessary to be clear about its purposes; and in this chapter I approach these purposes by considering what society needs or desires from the higher education system which it pays for. There is another approach, by considering what higher education does or should do for individuals, and this is deferred to the following chapter.

Medical practitioners require higher education. In Britain, the number pursuing medicine is largely determined by the allocation of resources to the National Health Service. Planning medical schools should therefore be easy: the data would be a reasonably long-term projection for the size of the Health Service, and information about the present age-structure of the profession and the likely wastage by retirement or transfer to other jobs. Despite this, we have suffered from severe shortages of doctors (particularly in certain specialist areas), and also from recurrent fears of possible over-production of medical graduates. Has this been due to mere incompetence in planning, or is there some deeper problem?

The example is a significant one, because some commentators would like to assume that higher education exists to provide specific manpower inputs to particular occupations, and should therefore be planned to yield these inputs. But if we fail in planning for so easy a case as medicine, what hope can we have of success for other subjects? No doubt there was an element of incompetence, as there was in the failure in the mid-1970s to match the supply of school teachers to the demand; but in fact the problem of doctor supply is by no means as easy as it looks. There is a very long time-lag between a decision to build a new medical school, or even to expand an existing one, and the related output of doctors. Government is neither willing nor able to give long-term projections of the size of the National Health Service, and guesses about trends therefore have to be substituted for facts. Part of the flow of doctors comes from the Irish Republic and from other places overseas, and part of the output of British medical schools will emigrate; the variations in the immigration and emigration rates can falsify the original assumptions. Serious shortages can arise in particular specialisms because the advantages, real or imagined, of joining them are seen to be less than in some other branch of medicine. The propensity of female doctors to continue work after marriage can alter, and probably has altered substantially in recent years. The extent of re-entry of married women doctors to the profession can vary. The assumptions about retirement may not be well-based. Finally, the elements of the model interact: for instance, the assumptions about the future resources of the Health Service are not independent of the number of doctors expected to be available to staff it.

The problems of planning teacher supply are no less difficult. The total number of teachers available for employment is not easy to estimate, because there are many married women who are qualified teachers and who would be attracted back to the profession if vacancies existed in the areas in which their husbands work. The number of teachers 'needed' is a function of decisions by local education authorities (and, at one remove, by government) about the desirable size of classes. It is generally assumed that the smaller classes are, the better the education given to the children (though there appears to be little confirmation of this from serious educational research). Naturally, therefore, the teachers' organizations react to proposals to reduce the flow of newly trained teachers by suggesting that the flow should be kept up and class sizes reduced. However, this solution of maintaining full employment by reducing (real or apparent) productivity is no help to government planners, who have to estimate how many teachers the Exchequer will be willing to pay for in ten or twenty years' time – that is, how fast staffing ratios can be improved. There is no hard basis of fact for making such an estimate.

Because of difficulties like these, the 'manpower planning' approach to the specification of higher education has been largely discredited. There are wider reasons why the discredit is deserved. A medical qualification does not usually lead to equivalent earnings in professions other than medicine, so it is broadly true to suppose that most trained doctors will follow medicine as a career. But other types of higher education, apparently specific in their vocational intention, are used – either at once, or at an indeterminate point later in working life – as an entry certificate to quite different occupations. Many accountants never practise accountancy, but go into general administration. Chemists often begin a career on specifically chemical work, but some then move to wider business responsibilities. These shifts between occupations vary according to relative attractions and to changes in demand and supply: they cannot therefore be accurately predicted from past statistics. In addition, of course, a large part of higher education is not tied to any specific vocation at all. It is possible to hold, as an extreme view, that all higher education *should* be vocational in its primary purpose, but this would certainly be a large change from what at present exists, and (because of the difficulty of defining the precise requirements of many vocations) it would almost certainly not be feasible.

Indeed, the cases like medicine, in which a particular course leads with a high probability to a particular occupation, are very much in the minority. Of the first-degree output of British universities, for instance, at most fifteen per cent comes from courses giving a fairly high probability of subsequent lifetime attachment to a particular occupation, about forty-five per cent comes from courses which the layman might regard as specifically vocational but which in fact lead to a variety of jobs, while forty per cent has an evidently low relationship to particular vocations.

So, forgetting the innocent dreams of the manpower planners, we must take another path. Society invests considerable resources in higher education, and evidently expects some benefit to follow. That benefit could be in the form of a more productive economic system, or at least one which manages to keep up with the advances of its international competitors. But it is difficult to prove that a particular level or type of higher education is (at the close of the twentieth century) necessary to economic success. Nothing can be deduced from the fact that rich nations spend a lot on higher education; this may simply be because they have rich resources to allocate, not because the allocation is a condition of their riches.

To make progress on this issue, one must first discard a careless but common habit of speech, namely to suggest that 'learning' is something which one does in a school or college or university, but not elsewhere. This is self-evident nonsense. All of us learn from experience, we learn by watching others, by private study and reading, by discovering and deducing things for ourselves; and, even where a formal act of teaching is needed, this is often provided 'on the job' by an employer. We should therefore reject any picture of the relationship of education to the economy which supposes that economic activity requires a set of exactly defined skills which must be provided in the right quantities by the educational system. The picture would be particularly misleading because the demands for skill are very likely to alter significantly during a man or woman's working life, and it would not be much use to be 'programmed' by education to meet a single specification, like a fixed logic circuit.

What an efficient economy needs, then, is a supply of people with a range of skills and an extent of understanding which will make them capable both of rapid learning of an initial task and of subsequent adaptation to changing demands. The concept of 'extent of understanding' involves two elements. One is the appreciation of basic principles, scientific laws, or statistical associations in the main field of interest. Thus it is not necessary to teach a man exactly how to operate or repair all the various forms of a particular machine, provided that he knows the principles on which it works and can therefore, faced with a practical problem, proceed quickly towards the answer. Equally, an intending business man need not memorise the Finance Acts, but he needs an understanding of the general principles of the tax system, so that he can know when to seek further information and advice about some budgetary change.

The other aspect of 'understanding' can be described as knowing enough, in related fields, to be able to recognise one's ignorance. This is standing on its head the idea that 'a little learning is a dangerous thing'. In fact, a little learning about a large number of matters is very necessary. There are not many simple single-discipline problems in an advanced economy, and although the larger organizations deal with the complexity by using teams of experts, these experts have to know enough about each other's specialisms to be able to interact properly. What is needed is an attachment to reality at many different points: a sufficiency of imaginative understanding of a range of problems, so that where necessary a deeper insight can be obtained. The need for this can be illustrated by some of our failures in foreign trade, and perhaps also in diplomacy, which have been caused by ignorance of the history, culture, religion, social structure and points of sensitivity of another nation, and by a crude transplantation of British preconceptions to another shore.

It used to be a popular idea in business that the basic skills, principles and understandings could be achieved in a good secondary school education, and that by the age of eighteen people are ready for the experience of 'real life', so that the usual period of higher education is a costly waste of time. Business men believed, and some still believe, that they could more appropriately provide the necessary higher training 'on the job', and that the final product would be better educated, at least in the limited sense of being of economic value, than the man or woman who came in after a period of higher education. This view is not necessarily ridiculous, and it is not disproved by observing that the demand for graduates has been rising; for if the system selects its best people to go on to take a degree, employers who want the best people may have to seek graduates, whatever their hesitations about the value of a degree. There is, in fact, no reliable way of proving that the economic 'requirement' for graduates (that is, the demand which employers would show for workers with a degree, if they could ignore considerations of supply and simply consider what will best improve the operation of their organizations and of the economy) is very high or rapidly increasing. The success of an economy is certainly related to the supply of first-class, original, energetic minds, and it is a matter for proper concern that the higher education system should be extremely efficient in selecting the first-rate people and in developing their valuable qualities further. The *economic* advantage of adding more graduates (or HND holders, or possessors of a professional qualification) who are essentially pedestrian and third-rate is unproved, though, as we shall see, there may be important individual and social advantages. The needs of the economy are relevant in considering the *content* of higher education, but they do not prove the need for it to be a mass activity.

What happens in practice is that conventions are established about the types of preparation for economic activity which are given in institutions of higher education, and the types best provided by the employer or by private study. From time to time, occupations shift from the second group to the first. This movement, however, may not be due to any superior excellence of full-time institutional preparation. It may, as suggested above, be due to a growing social custom, pushing the more able down the tramlines of higher education, or it may be due to the realization by employers that it is very much cheaper to leave their training costs to the state. On the other hand, there will certainly be areas of advanced skill and understanding, and particularly those which are minority rather than mass interests, for which it is much better to rely on full-time education rather than a patchwork of special efforts by employers.

One should thus not believe those who assert that a vast expansion of higher education is essential to economic salvation;

they usually turn out to be interested parties. A more careful approach suggests that the economic requirements are significant in considering the *content* of higher education – a point to which I revert on p. 62 – but that, beyond the need to develop the first-rate, and not to frustrate or to misdirect them, conclusions about numbers must be much more tentative. Nor can one prove a need for universities because economic progress needs fundamental research. The relation between amounts of basic research and economic success is very slender – the key is not original discovery, but skill in carrying through a timely exploitation. Nor does research have to be in teaching institutions; it could be segregated in special research establishments. There is a strong belief in universities, in particular, that research enlivens teaching, though, as I suggest in Chapter 8, even this is probably due to an inexact use of the word 'research'. The obverse proposition, that teaching enlivens research, will certainly not do as a generalization, though one can identify some special cases where it is plausible.

It is time, however, to pay heed to those who regard the economic success of the country as a secondary issue, something which is not as important as the happiness of its citizens or its cultural or spiritual development, and which is not the necessary or sufficient condition for these greater forms of good. This way of looking at things has implications for the needs of individuals, which are discussed in the next chapter, but it also suggests an alternative formulation of the benefit which society finds in higher education. This benefit would be the maintenance and enrichment of national culture; or, if you like, the enrichment of world culture and the perfection of the sub-culture of the national area.

The word 'culture' must here be used in a meaning much wider than a collection of works of art and literature. It implies that in the whole patchwork of human activity, playing Beethoven, racing greyhounds, climbing mountains, testing chemicals, building houses, solving mathematical problems, conducting political affairs – and so on, and so on – it is possible to make judgements about what is worth *remembering:* what we would like to pass as a legacy to our successors, as a foundation on which they can build even better things. The 'enrichment' of culture can thus be seen as the joint effect of raising the average quality and of diversifying still further, often by bringing in, and adopting as our own, forms of activity which began in other countries, but sometimes by inventing entirely new ventures.

It can be argued, of course, that on many matters there are no absolute standards of better and worse, and therefore no basis for a judgement on what should be remembered. I happen to believe, for instance, that the standards of modern British art and architecture are deplorably low; but obviously the practitioners do not think so, and they will have many supporters who will regard my viewpoint as uncultured and old-fashioned. But the fact is that, though distinctions among the second-rate are hard to make, greatness comes with its own convincing power. Very few people would be found to disagree that Shakespeare, the Bible, the institution of parliamentary democracy, the Theory of Relativity, the (largely man-made) beauty of the Lake District, the development of scientific method, Handel's Messiah – all these things, and many more, belong with assurance to the list of those worth remembering.

Elements of culture can be preserved from complete loss by being written down, charted, photographed, recorded on tape, but this is not the same as giving them the remembrance they deserve. In the seventeenth and eighteenth centuries, for instance, the Bible was well known to people in every class of society, and this had an effect not only on faith, and perhaps on morals, but, because of the splendours of the Authorised Version, on the quality of language. Now the Bible is relatively unkown, and we are poorer as a consequence, even though other works of literature and other means of stimulating thought on fundamental issues have gained in familiarity. In fact, the maintenance of culture requires the serious study of its elements by a sufficient leavening group in each generation. Its enrichment from other cultures is similarly a learning process. Its improvement may sometimes seem to be spontaneous, but it depends on an acquired culture, however little it may seem to use its elements.

Society has an interest, therefore, in higher education as a means of providing the memory of civilization, and of giving, to a minority at least, an advanced knowledge of a part of our heritage and therefore a basis for new achievement. But this is not the limit of the non-economic interest. Citizenship in a complex society requires a high state of understanding of the way of working of that society – its faults and problems, as well as its achievements; its informal habits, as well as its formal institutions. A part of the investment in higher education is therefore an investment in more competent citizenship. It provides, in every generation, people in each locality who have had to think more deeply about the working of society, who have seen some of its problems in historical perspective, or in the light of research, or with the clarifying influence of philosophical discussion. It will be noted that these interests of society provide a powerful justification for equal opportunity for women: the educated unpaid housewife is fully as important as the educated paid worker.

But the proper purposes of higher education go beyond the preservation and understanding of past and present achievements. It is also an instrument of change. Those parts of higher education which are heavily involved in research create change as a consequence of new discovery. Teaching at degree level is sometimes designed to develop the critical and questioning mind: as it is often put, 'to make the student think for himself'. Such a process, allied to the natural propensity of the young to think little of their elders' achievements, creates reformers or even revolutionaries. It is presumably this contribution to which the Carnegie Commission refers (p. ix above) as 'the critical evaluation of society – through individual thought and persuasion – for the sake of society's self-renewal'. The same critical mind, employed not on the evaluation of society but on the received wisdom of science, gives rise to new ways of understanding the material world, which can have large practical consequences. Or, used to take apart and re-assess an industrial problem, it can lead to new solutions in technology.

It will be generally accepted as a good thing to have revolutionary ideas in physics or engineering, which can yield
useful results like better motor-cars or more versatile pocket
calculators. Society's view of those who develop critical
thoughts about the established order is much more ambiguous.
A certain amount of liveliness and lack of reverence is applauded,
but there is concern that it may increase in proportion to the
increase in higher education. If the critical faculty goes too far
it is seen as 'subversive', and people want to know why good
taxpayers' money is being spent on the support of dangerous
revolutionaries. This defensive reaction should not be con-
demned out of hand, for some of those regarded as 'subversive'
have developed a singularly lop-sided critical faculty, analysing
and condemning the existing order, while holding with a religious fervour to an unquestioned political dogma – just as
some supporters of the 'establishment' condemn all its critics
without being willing to look seriously at the faults of present
society. The view which we ought to take is that society should
encourage and protect the even-handed pursuit of truth
wherever it may lead, even though this may be a disturbing
thing to do; and that it should welcome the development of
independent critical thinking, by a teaching influence which
encourages impartial criticism of all positions.

But this view, like some others explained in this chapter,
belongs to the more enlightened or thoughtful members of
the community. A random sample of citizens, asked why
higher education is provided, would probably give as a majority
answer 'To prepare people for jobs' – which, as we have seen,
is no satisfactory answer at all. A rather more sophisticated
view is that it makes the country richer; this is not an adequate
answer, but it does tell us something about the desirable
content of the education. The preservation and development
of culture, the discovery of new facts and ideas, the development
of a properly critical spirit – these are what we *ought* to desire,
but there are probably few votes to be got from supporting
such ideas. Yet it should be noted that the 'enlightened' view
of society's need for higher education is not far removed from

the ambitions of many students for their personal development: which leads us to the subject of the next chapter.

3
THE NEEDS AND DESIRES
OF THE INDIVIDUAL

The Robbins report (*Higher Education*, Cmnd. 2154, 1963), having found it impracticable to estimate overall manpower requirements – beyond saying that the country needed 'a great increase in the present provision of places in higher education' – took refuge in the principle that 'all young persons qualified by ability and attainment to pursue a full-time course in higher education should have the opportunity to do so'. The main use made of the principle was to derive estimates of future numbers – though, considering the vagueness of the words 'qualified by ability and attainment', and the uncertainty about the proportion of young persons who would use the opportunity granted, these estimates got more attention than they deserved. But the statement of the principle, and its implicit acceptance by government, had the important effect of creating a new individual 'right'. The report sees this right to higher education as justified by the need to 'make the most of the talents of citizens' in order to achieve economic ends, and to fulfil the 'aspirations of a modern community as regards both wealth and culture'. It also saw it as 'characteristic of the aspirations of this age' that where there is capacity to understand, to contemplate and to create, that capacity should be fostered.

The resounding phrases of the report conceal a certain sloppiness of thinking. The economic justification for a large increase was not as self-evident as the Committee supposed; and its apparent belief that the community avidly desired a higher standard of culture was unsupported by evidence. The fostering of the capacities of citizens sounds like an aim as uncontroversial as being in favour of virtue; but what the Report was about was the spending of a lot of money on fostering the capacities of a select group of citizens, mainly in a particular age-group. Resources are scarce, and often have alternative uses, so it may be that the right to a better school education, or the right to continued education through adult life, or the right to a better environment or better health care, should have taken priority.

Indeed, it is questionable whether a 'right' to resources can properly exist, in any way comparable to other rights which we seek to establish, such as freedom under the law or absence of discrimination on grounds of race or sex. A right to resources implies a judgement that a particular activity has permanent priority, however limited the resources and however urgent the competing claims. What the Robbins Committee should have said, I think, is: 'Our judgement is that the country can and should afford, during the period 1963–1983, to provide higher education for young people whose attainments are comparable to those of recent entrants to degree courses, and who wish to take up the opportunity'.

There would be little difficulty in making a similar promise for the next twenty years, since the fall in the birth rate suggests the possibility of a reduction in the resources used. But what are the needs which we should really be trying to meet, for the rest of this century and beyond?

The evidence suggests that, on a human population born with diverse inherited abilities, there operates a cumulative and powerful social effect, such that those brought up in lower social class homes have on average much lower educational attainments, and are relatively less likely to complete a sixth form course. This constitutes a waste of ability, and calls (on grounds both of social justice and of national good house-keeping) for urgent and vigorous remedial action. But that action must mainly be taken in the homes and in the schools; by definition, it belongs to the levels below higher education. Higher education institutions could contribute remedial courses (as I recommend on p. 54-5), but in doing so they would be doing work below that which we have called 'higher'.

The students who come from the sixth forms are thus a select sample, perhaps with special characteristics, of the more able children born into lower social class families, and a much larger sample of the children of the managerial and professional classes. (The class bias is to some extent lessened by the provision of opportunities for adult students, but there are practical limitations to the ability of adult students to take years off in mid-career.) The needs of students differ greatly according to these differences in background: some will be widely read, others will have read little; some will have travelled abroad, others will seldom have left their home town; some will have been to schools rich in resources and tradition, others to schools which are poorly staffed and which have no great interest in higher education. In some homes the habits of hard work are acquired early and naturally, and in others they are not acquired at all.

These are variations superimposed on personality differences. Some students are self-propelling, endowed with an intellectual curiosity and enthusiasm which carries them forward with minimal assistance from their teachers. Others require to be pushed every inch of the way. Some gain in clarity of mind and in ability to concentrate when faced by a difficult task; others become confused and anxious, and, as we so often say, 'fail to do themselves justice'. It is a proper criticism of our higher education system that, though some differences of method exist between its parts, each institution tends to apply to its students a teaching method much more standardized than is appropriate to the variability of its human material.

But what are we trying to do to this varied material? The usual answer from teachers in higher education is about the development of higher-level cognitive skills, such as extrapolation, the use of abstractions, analysis and synthesis, the examination of consistency, the judgement of results by external criteria. In the inexact common speech, the student must think clearly and 'think for himself' – that is, deduce new things from his existing knowledge or ideas. He (or she) must also show a proper acquaintance with the methods and material of the chosen subject or subjects; but there is suspicion of a large amount of 'rote learning', and the stress is on being able to *use* the methods on new material and to *find out* new facts, rather than on being able to reproduce a standard text-book. Particular value is often seen to exist in those who can obtain fresh insight by bringing together the methods or materials of different subjects.

The Carnegie Commission definition of purposes, quoted in the Prologue, is however wider; it refers to the 'intellectual, aesthetic, ethical, and skill development of individual students'. The Commission (p. 14) found that (subject to the uncertainties which always attach to surveys of opinion) 'undergraduate students themselves place a particularly high priority on the following and in this general order:

Their 'emotional growth'
'Learning to get along with people'
'Formation of values and goals'
'A detailed grasp of a special field'
'A well-rounded general education'
'Training and skills for an occupation'
'Outlets for creative activities'
'Earning power' '

This list may be influenced by some special features of United States culture, but it is nevertheless highly significant that the purposes which relate to intellectual development appear, not on the top, but in the middle of the list, and are preceded by purposes which involve ethical, social and emotional development.

What lies behind this is the realization that intellectual development is not enough: that it does not, as a matter of fact, enable people to be more successful in facing the common difficulties and troubles of life, and may indeed stand in the way of this success; that it does not necessarily lead to greater happiness, nor even to greater effectiveness in making a contribution to society. The demand is that higher education should provide an all-round development, and not leave the fostering of qualities other than cognitive skills to chance. This is a very proper demand, and it would be difficult to produce any sound justification of the preoccupation of educators with intellectual skills alone. But, if we accept a wider definition of the needs of the individual, there will be substantial implications for the content and method of higher education; some of these are explored in later chapters. It should be noted, too, that – though 'creative activities' do not get a very high priority in the Carnegie list – all-round development implies an attention to aesthetic sensitivity and to creative abilities, and these too tend to be underrated, or confined to specialist groups of students, in present systems of higher education.

The low place occupied by 'earning power' in the Carnegie list may be a reflection of abundant employment opportunities open to American students at the time. There is certainly evidence in British experience, since the advent of higher unemployment in the mid-1970s, of a sharp swing towards vocational courses, and in particular those which are thought to offer security, good earnings, or early promotion. The choice of courses by students is in fact volatile, and appears often to be related to some on-intellectual aspect of a subject. Thus, the desire to 'get along with people' is evidenced in the number of students who say 'I want to work with people'. They suppose, wrongly of course, that science and engineering careers are mostly about 'things', and therefore crowd into subjects like social administration and psychology. The search for something which will make sense, in a comprehensive way, of the problems of life is expressed as a demand for 'relevance'; and at various times subjects such as philosophy, sociology, politics and religious studies are seen as providing this relevance. Perhaps a vague sense of aesthetic longing, or a feeling of being starved for culture, may explain the large numbers who choose English Literature as a subject. Possibly, however, the large numbers are explained by the belief that the subject is a 'soft option', in which reasonable success may be obtained without severe intellectual effort. It is indeed necessary to admit that one explanation of student choice is that it is a self-interested reaction to rumours that one subject is a softer option than another, or that one subject leads more readily than another to a 'status' which the student admires.

All this takes us a long way from the Robbins criterion. This was based on a 'qualification by ability and attainment', which was generally taken to refer to a measure of success in the Advanced level of the General Certificate of Education, and on a subsequent choice by the student to take up the opportunity in higher education. But if the educational needs of students are wider than the development of higher-level cognitive skills, an entry test related to cognitive skills is not self-evidently appropriate; it certainly will not give the receiving institution a proper indication of the way in which it should adapt courses and methods to the real needs and qualities of the student. And if the choice of what to do in higher education is based on vague and volatile yearnings, which get associated with this subject or that, there must be serious doubt about the rationality of the prior choice of whether to go into higher education at all.

There are serious shortcomings in Advanced level examinations, and (so far as is known) in any of the alternative sixth-form-level tests, even as measures of intellectual competence. They perform reasonably well as predictors of subsequent examination success in mathematics and mathematically-based subjects, but rather badly in the humanities and social sciences; so there is an existing mismatch between what is thought to be a desirable test of success in sixth-form work, and what teachers in higher education consider to be needed for their courses. A prolonged effort to develop new entry tests of scholastic aptitude, similar to those used in the United States, yielded no decided advantage. In the light of the discussion in this chapter, there seem to be two ways forward. One is to develop a better and more comprehensive battery of tests, which could be used not only to assess cognitive skills but also wider needs, and which could have a diagnostic purpose in enabling the university or college to determine just what curriculum and teaching method will suit the needs of a particular student. The other is to admit that all such testing is exceedingly difficult, so that the choice of entrants will to some extent remain arbitrary, and that the choice *by* entrants (to go into higher education, and to select a particular place and a particular course) is necessarily ill-informed because of their lack of experience. Therefore students who succeed in a test rather simpler than A-level (and perhaps confined to basic cognitive skills) should be admitted to higher education, if they so wish, for an experimental period, in which they can make a more rational choice and the institution can assess their wider need.

This freedom to 'have a go' is at present hard to find, even for students who intend to study in their spare time. The Open University has a restriction on the number of its entrants. The professional bodies increasingly set entrance requirements to their courses which are as restrictive as those of the higher education institutions. But I do not think it very likely that we shall succeed in making the right decisions by yet more subtle testing; and the problem will become a more difficult one as we seek to do justice to the less 'academic' students in the new sixth forms. Therefore one of the changes which would be desirable, over the next twenty years, is an increased opportunity to test what higher education has to offer, without undue restriction from inappropriate entrance tests.

Overall, what we seek as an ideal is a structure comprehensive enough to meet the whole needs of individuals, whether cognitive or otherwise; flexible enough to meet the great variations in those needs, from person to person; and intelligible enough to enable a rational choice to be made. In succeeding chapters we begin the search for this structure. To the extent that the search can be successful, it will provide not only for the greater satisfaction of the needs and desires of individuals, but also for a better match to the requirements of society. For neither the economic nor the cultural needs of society, nor its need of enlightened citizenship, are well served by unbalanced intellectuals inadequately developed in the ethical, social and emotional areas.

4
LEVELS AND PATTERNS

The higher education institutions of Britain, described in Chapter 1, contain many variations. The 'level' reached by students varies from diplomas below degree standard, through first degrees, to Masters' degrees and doctorates. In addition, many short courses are provided which fall within the definition of 'higher education' set out in the Prologue. The intensity of work required to succeed differs to some extent, though not enough to match the great differences in the students coming forward. There are three- and four-year full-time first degrees, and longer part-time degrees, including those of the Open University. There are one- and two-year Masters' degrees, and a great variation in the time taken (in practice) to obtain a doctorate. Some places teach many subjects, and others only a few; some are much concerned with science and technology, or with social science, or professional or business studies, or the humanities, while others aim at a balance of all these. There are institutions dedicated to teaching, with little or no research, and others with a heavy commitment to research. There are institutions which go only as far as a first degree, and others with graduate schools. Types of teaching vary, with different patterns of use of small-group teaching – and with the Open University as a special case, with its own teaching style. The hours of contact between student and teacher vary greatly between subjects, but also substantially between institutions for the same subject. Patterns of student living vary, some places being largely residential and drawing students from all over the United Kingdom and from all over the world, while others have a regional interest, and yet others rely mainly on students who live at home and travel daily. Some places close down, and most of the staff disappear, when 'holidays' arrive; others have found continuing functions at almost all times of the year.

The last point apart, nearly all of this variety is desirable, and indeed still more variety is needed to match the diversity of human beings and the multiplicity of society's needs. But there is no systematic or logical relation between the differences of practice and the differences between types of institution. To put the matter more precisely, while there are of course differences of practice between universities, polytechnics, colleges of higher education, and so on, these differences are often less than those existing *between* universities, or *between* polytechnics, or *between* other colleges. In consequence, there is a great deal of overlap between the various sectors, and many of the generalizations about their characteristics which one meets turn out to be false. As we have seen (p. 9), it is not a valid generalization that polytechnics are more concerned with 'applied' studies than universities, or that they act more speedily in response to national needs. Nor is it a valid generalization that universities are more effective in teaching than colleges of higher education, even though they have the advantage in attracting able staff and in the multiplicity of their resources.

Inevitably, a collection of institutions so varied, with divided ownership and differing access to funds, is open to allegations of waste. In the same city, two half-empty technology departments compete for students – why not close one department down? Why build up libraries adequate to support both teaching and research in over forty institutions, and major teaching libraries in many more, so that often several large libraries will be found within a few miles of each other? Why not use the very best teachers to lecture to as many students as can be brought together to hear them – or perhaps, through film and television, to have their effect nation-wide? If the Open University has painstakingly, and with first-rate technical advice on the effective use of media, constructed a course on the calculus or Marxian economics or Spanish, why should a host of inexperienced and ill-supported lecturers need to invent their own courses? Why pay a boy from Aberdeen to travel to Sussex, and live there in a hall of residence, when a course in his chosen subject is available at a short bus-ride from his parents' home? Why should a small country support over seventy graduate schools, many having, for particular subjects, resources which are ludicrously inadequate?

There certainly seem to be enough questions of this kind to give rise to a presumption that better planning is needed. However, the case for this is not quite as good as it may appear. Some of the chosen examples of waste conceal assumptions which should be questioned. The two half-empty departments may be offering quite different versions of their subject, and it may be desirable that both should be kept in being. A Sussex course in, say, sociology may be very different from one in Aberdeen, and the student may have good reason for choosing one rather than the other. Even if the courses do not differ greatly, the Aberdeen boy's background may be such that his educational development will be much more rapid if he leaves home; the extra cost of keeping him in Sussex may be in reality a wise economy. Education is not just a matter of lectures, and television presentations (however expert) are often not as effective as personal contact with a teacher. Furthermore, what is called 'waste' is sometimes better described as creative rivalry. A fully planned system will embody the mistakes made by the planners, and will be hard to change because the planners will be unwilling to admit to error. It may be very much worth while to tolerate overlapping and a multiplicity of effort, in order to make sure that new ideas can emerge.

These are arguments similar to those used to suggest that, in a free enterprise economy, the harm done by occasional waste or overlapping is less important than the benefits derived from free initiative. The same point can be made in another way. The arguments for a planned system are essentially arguments for specialization of function, so that each task of teaching, and presumably also of research, is performed at an efficient scale. There would be two departments offering degrees in Russian, instead of thirty or so, and only one of the two would provide for higher degree work. Library resources for Russian studies could thus be limited to two institutions. If twenty departments of physics survived, students could be directed to attend, if at all possible, one within daily travelling distance of their parental home, thus saving a lot of money.

But such a plan would give rise to two difficulties. First, subjects are not independent of each other; they are indeed made fruitful by their interaction. Universities and colleges will want to go on providing degree programmes which involve several subjects, even though this involves doing some teaching at what appears to be less than an optimum scale. Second, specialization by institution implies that the student *either* chooses the right place to go to (and thereafter does not change his mind) *or* is free to move to another appropriately specialized institution if he finds he has made the wrong choice. But the evidence suggests that choices are often made badly, and preferences often change during the early months of study. Furthermore, mobility has hitherto been difficult to arrange, and it is unpopular with students – indeed, it may be harmful, for it breaks social ties which themselves have an educational value. Thus the wide spread of activities commonly found within institutions or classes of institutions may be seen as the necessary condition of adapting their service to the variability and mutability of the human mind. This is implicitly acknowledged by the use of the term 'monotechnic' as a form of disparagement.

From time to time, suggestions are made about a 'comprehensive' system of higher education. This is a dangerously misleading term, because it invites comparison with the comprehensive school system. A school which includes children under the minimum school leaving age can be called 'comprehensive' because education is compulsory, and the school aims to provide for virtually the whole range of ability and interest in the age-groups which it covers. No-one suggests that higher education could or should be compulsory, and by definition it does *not* provide for the whole range of ability.

What the protagonists of a 'comprehensive' system of higher education mean is that, within the defined field of higher education, institutions or linked groups of institutions should provide all types of course; one and two-year courses as well as degree courses, a full range of subject options, part-time as well as full-time courses, and so on. It is not enough that these options should exist somewhere within the entire national provision of higher education, for this does not fully or effectively allow opportunities to move from one course to another. Therefore it is suggested, for instance, that, within a region of manageable size, all the universities and colleges should be brought into some form of federation, students becoming, so to speak, 'citizens' of the federation with freedom to move anywhere within it. (This federation proposal is more practical than the idea that a single institution should provide every kind of course, which would imply units of enormous size.) Some people see in their 'comprehensive' proposals the added advantage that they would promote 'parity of esteem' for all the providers of courses, and break down the social superiority of the universities. Experience suggests, however, that the human tendency to establish a pecking order for different institutions is not likely to be easily forgotten.

There is a considerable danger that a federation of the type described would be the enemy of excellence. Indeed, the supporters of the idea sometimes seem to be moved by envy of the superior facilities of the universities, and might well wish to spread the available funds, and the use of existing resources such as buildings and libraries, more evenly over the members of the federation, even if they thereby damaged the special contribution of the universities. There would be a danger, too, that a complex bureaucracy would arise, obstructing the free development of new ideas. Forms of government would have to be adapted, to fit in with the requirements of the federation, and in the process valuable freedoms might be lost.

These are arguments which are strong enough to make most people – especially those in universities – prefer the existing state of affairs, even if it leads to some waste and occasionally fails to provide the best opportunities for the advancement of students. I am myself now convinced that the 'comprehensive' idea is too dangerous to be worth further consideration. This is not only because it is likely to be promoted from the wrong motives. A more fundamental difficulty is that it would be hard to run a large federation, with free movement of students within it, without creating a tendency to uniformity of provision and method. I do not want to solve the problems of poorly-endowed institutions by levelling-down their partners in the federation, nor to make life easier for weak students by reducing the challenge to the more able. In the British context, a particular difficulty is that the universities do not regard themselves as regional institutions; this does not imply an unwillingness to help near neighbours, but the student body is commonly drawn from a very wide geographical area. This suggests that co-ordination of resources and offerings would only be possible if done at national level – where it would be a very complex task.

But a conclusion unfavourable to the 'comprehensive' federation has to be reached with regret. It is a pity, for instance, that no-one has the duty to ask the question whether the mix of facilities provided in, say, Greater Manchester is an appropriate fit to the need. In fact, as we shall see in the next chapter, there is a presumption that, both regionally and nationally, the fit is very far from appropriate. It is a pity that more should not be done to make common use of resources, and to open to students wider opportunities than can be provided in a single college.

It will be seen from Chapter 1, however, that instruments of planning and co-ordination already exist for the public sector colleges. The Regional Advisory Councils and HM Inspectors concern themselves with overlapping provision; the validating bodies (and in particular the Council for National Academic Awards) necessarily have an interest in the adequacy of the resources for the courses they approve, and therefore in the proper use of the resources available in an area. I suggested in

Chapter 1 that so far no strong evidence exists of the virtues
of this planning, and doubts about its value are supported by
the arguments of the last few pages. Nevertheless, it is worth
considering whether a better and more comprehensive system
of planning would yield benefits which would outweigh its
disadvantages.

The search for such a system was part of the remit of the
Working Group on the Management of Higher Education
in the Maintained Sector (the Oakes Committee), which
reported in March 1978. It was charged to 'consider measures
to improve the system of management and control of higher
education in the maintained sector in England and Wales and
its better coordination with higher education in the universities'.
Those who set up the Group evidently supposed that better
planning and co-ordination were needed, partly because of
the large amounts of money now being spent on public sector
higher education, and the Group itself accepted this. It seems
to have supposed that co-ordination with the universities
could be achieved by inviting voluntary co-operation on
regional councils, and by close discussion with the UGC,
the extent of that body's power to influence academic matters
being, one suspects, greatly overestimated. But the most
interesting outcome was that, within the maintained and public
sectors, the proposals as they emerged were for a form of
planning too weak to be likely to have much new effect.

The Committee proposed the creation of a new National
Body (later described as two Advanced Further Education
Councils for England and for Wales) which would collect
information, advise the Secretary of State and the local authorities on the total provision needed, issue guidance on programmes and estimates submitted, allocate funds (or advise on their
allocation), and have general oversight of the development
of maintained higher education and its cost-effectiveness.
Nine new regional advisory councils would be established,
covering the whole public sector. So far this sounds like a
formidable apparatus of control, but the picture looks rather
different when one examines the financial proposals. Three

methods of finance were suggested: *per capita* payments for students, which were considered appropriate for courses of local and regional interest and for advanced courses in institutions mainly engaged in non-advanced work; payment of the full cost of a course; and programme finance (i.e. a consolidated grant) for major institutions.

The full-cost method, which would require specific course approval, is regarded as an exception to be used in a minority of cases. The *per capita* payment method would not involve formal course approval, the influence of the Regional Advisory Councils (which is already exercised) being considered a sufficient safeguard against waste when associated with the proposal (p. 12) that local authorities should themselves meet from five to fifteen per cent of the costs locally arising; they would thus bear a modest burden if they authorized courses which were expensive in relation to the *per capita* payment. For the major institutions, however, programme support would be appropriate; and this would follow approval of the broad heads of a programme, with accompanying estimates, the institution being left with 'considerable discretion' within these heads, including 'varying the detailed provision of courses and students to be recruited'. It would be expected to remember the interests of neighbouring institutions, by consultation within the Regional Advisory Council. Such a system could certainly be operated in a more interventionist way than that taken by the University Grants Committee, but, given the strong desire for autonomy in powerful local authorities and their major institutions, is likely to fall far short of providing effective regional or national plans for the logical distribution of course provision.

In the light of the doubts expressed earlier in this chapter, the weaker the planning mechanism, the better: for an effective and tight system of national planning would be the enemy of free initiative and variety. Until we find planners who are sensitive to the need for variety and who welcome new ideas even if they have not initiated them, the present arrangement with overlapping ranges of activities and functions for each type of institution is probably the best. It provides us with a multiplicity of 'growing points', and enough competition to keep people on their toes. It has not, however, provided us with enough variety of levels and periods of higher education; this is a matter to be explored in the next chapter.

5

INSTITUTIONAL STRUCTURE
IN THE YEAR 2000

I suggested in Chapter 3 (p. 35) that we should seek a structure comprehensive enough to meet the whole needs of individuals, but also flexible and intelligible. The implication of Chapter 4 is that such a structure should not be planned centrally and imposed, but should grow naturally and admit of the possibility of overlapping and competition. Nevertheless the influence of government on the manner of that growth is necessarily great; for instance, certain types of course are unlikely to appear while the present rules about the eligibility of students for grants remain unchanged. It is not good enough, therefore, to let the structure of the year 2000 be a natural growth within present constraints and subject to present inducements. We need to think how the constraints and the inducements should be changed, so as to get us nearer to our ideal structure.

There is an evident gap in the system now existing, in relation to our definition of higher education as building on, and going beyond, sixth form studies. Sixth forms of schools have always included students whose extent of preparation and spread of learning are insufficient to make it wise for them to go on to a full degree course. The proportion of such students is likely to increase, with the growth of sixth forms in a changing secondary school system. In years past, by a historical accident which was permitted to be influential for too long, students of lesser ability, and particularly girls, were allowed to have an opportunity of higher education in a teachers' training college. Belatedly it has been realized that school teaching is far too important to be left to recruit from the lower levels of attainment; but the move to graduate teacher education has left only limited opportunities of full-time higher education below degree level. One effort to create such an opportunity, the Diploma of Higher Education (a two-year course) was still-born because of an extraordinary decision that it should have the same minimum entrance requirements (that is, two passes in the Advanced level of the General Certificate of Education) as a degree. Part-time vocational courses exist abundantly, of course, in the further education system, but they cannot generally be regarded as providing a full general education, nor is this their intention. Entry to full-time further education courses is made more difficult by the uncertainties of the grant system.

Unless the distribution of ability has an unexpected kink, it would be expected that the number of students capable of benefiting by two years of study beyond the sixth form would exceed those capable of benefiting by three or four years, and that the number capable of benefiting by one year would be greater still. It does not follow, of course, that provision should be made in exact accordance with this distribution, though there is a presumption that the demand of society for developed skills may have a similar shape – that is, for every hundred graduates we need more than a hundred sub-graduate 'technicians'. If one concentrates on *full-time* education, there are plausible reasons for giving lower priority to one-year programmes, which would tend to be inefficient because of the waste of time and energy in settling into a new institution; inducements to remain for a third year in the sixth form might be better.

It is difficult, however, to gainsay the need for a much greater provision of two-year full-time courses (or the equivalent in part-time study), if the system is to be comprehensive enough in meeting the needs of individuals. It is relevant that in the United States the junior or community colleges have grown greatly in number in recent years, providing (on one estimate) almost half of the campuses and for more than half of all the students in the first two years of higher education. Their function can be defined as 'postsecondary education that offers one of several opportunities: career preparation for middle-level managerial or technical employment; first-cycle study, usually comprising the first two years of a university education; continuing general education; development and remedial education; or community service.' (*International Encyclopaedia of Higher Education*, San Francisco: Jossey-Bass, 1977, vol. 8, p. 3820, under *Short-cycle education.*) Three elements of this are underdeveloped in the British system: the opportunity to test abilities in higher education without a long-term commitment (see p. 35), and then (if the student wishes and has shown an adequate performance) to transfer to a degree course; the opportunity to remedy deficiencies in earlier education, which can be particularly important to racial minorities; and (above all) the opportunity to extend and develop general education, in two year courses.

High on the list of priorities for the year 2000, therefore, I put the development of a nation-wide system of community colleges offering two-year full-time courses (though no doubt also offering the part-time equivalent, and also a range of shorter courses both for initial entrants and for adults). Students on these courses should be grant-aided in the same way as those on degree courses. Such a system of colleges could come into being in part by developing a greater range of interest in existing further education colleges, particularly in general education, and in part by using the spare capacity which has appeared in the teacher training system, though this would imply changes in the outlook of college of education staff. The development of new opportunities for the product of the new sixth forms would be a far more valuable use of this spare capacity than the recent attempts to copy university courses. However, the logic of a community college system which provides both terminal two-year courses and also a route into degree courses is that the number of places needed in the degree-giving institutions will be lower. At present there is pressure on students to attempt degree courses for which they may be ill-qualified by attainment, or for which their motivation is uncertain. Many teachers in universities and colleges would be glad to be able to advise such students to seek a less demanding course, while still keeping open the opportunity to transfer to the degree stream. The implication of needing fewer degree places, in a period which is likely in any case to see declining enrolments for demographic reasons, is that some of the existing degree institutions might be available either for conversion into pure community colleges, or, more likely, for development into a 'comprehensive' institution with a two-year college for general education within it. This type of comprehensiveness was, indeed, part of the original idea of the polytechnics, but many have sought to escape from 'lower level' work, and there have been few cases of imaginative development of two-year general education, as distinct from vocational courses.

In general, the community colleges would be non-residential, so the number required would be determined by possibilities of daily travel. There should, however, be some partly residential colleges, to avoid injustice to rural areas, and to provide for students who doubt the possibility of satisfactory study when based at home. (The problems of differential grants for resident and non-resident students would be eased by recourse to a partial loan system: see p. 116 below). The number of colleges should not be allowed to exceed the minimum demanded by the geographical spread of population, since the aim would be to bring within each college a sufficient range of subjects and courses to allow students a reasonable chance of changing their minds, and, perhaps more important, to give them the opportunity of frequent meeting with people of interests different from their own. The disappearance, apart from a few special cases, of the 'monotechnic' college – such as the old-style teacher training colleges, in which all students were committed to the same profession and studied only with others so committed – has been a desirable change.

I have put the community college proposal first in this chapter because it relates to the most striking misfit between the potential of those with sixth form education, or the equivalent, and the provision made for them. It is not of course true overall that the choice has been 'a degree or nothing', but in particular non-technical subject areas this is certainly how the choice has appeared to many students. Furthermore there has been a strong tendency among the degree-course institutions to become more uniform in the average *level* of their offerings, despite all the competitive diversity of the content. Polytechnics have reduced lower-level work, developed graduate studies and research, and become more like universities. Higher education colleges have produced degree courses closely resembling those in universities. It is necessary to ask, therefore, whether some greater differentiation, at levels above that of the community college, is desirable in order to give a better fit to the variations of ability while still preserving an efficient use of resources.

The United States example is interesting here also; not because we should always follow the Americans, but because the complex higher education system of that country represents something like a natural growth in response to community demands, and can perhaps reveal the detail of those demands more effectively than our own smaller and more regulated system. The Carnegie Council (successor to the Commission) classifies institutions as follows:

1   *Research universities I (51)*

   Those included among the 50 leading universities in terms of federal financial support of academic science in at least two of a period of three years – provided also that in the middle year they awarded at least 50 Ph.D.s (or M.D.s if a medical school was on the same campus).

2   *Research universities II (47)*

   Those either *among the first 100 in federal financial support, with 50 Ph.D.s or M.D.s (at least 25 Ph.D.s)* or *among the leading 60 Ph.D.-granting institutions over a ten year period;* or *otherwise qualified by impressive graduate programmes.*

3   *Doctorate-granting universities I (56)*
    Those awarding 40 or more Ph.D.s in at least five
    fields; or receiving in one of two years at least $3
    million federal support.

4   *Doctorate-granting universities II (30)*
    Those awarding at least 20 Ph.D.s without regard
    to field, or 10 Ph.D.s in at least three fields.

5   *Comprehensive universities and colleges I (381)*
    Institutions over 2000 students with at least two
    professional or occupational courses as well as liberal
    arts degrees. Many offer masters' degrees, but
    doctoral programmes are absent or very small.

6   *Comprehensive universities and colleges II (213)*
    Institutions over 1500 (private) or 1000 (public),
    with at least one professional programme as well as
    liberal arts degrees.

7   *Liberal Arts colleges I (123)*
    So classified either by the quality of their intake or by
    the number of their graduates who subsequently
    obtain Ph.D.s elsewhere.

8   *Liberal Arts colleges II (460)*
    All other liberal arts (that is, predominantly non-
    professional) colleges.

9   *Two-year colleges and institutes (1147)*

10 *Separate professional schools and other specialized*
    institutions (560)

11 *Institutions for non-traditional study (6)*

The numbers in brackets show how many institutions fell

into each category in 1976. Only twenty-seven per cent of the enrolment was in the doctorate-granting universities (classes 1 to 4); twenty-eight per cent was in the 'comprehensive universities and colleges' (classes 5 and 6); five per cent in liberal arts colleges; and nearly forty per cent in the rest. (See *A Classification of Institutions of Higher Education*, revised edition, 1976: Carnegie Council on Policy Studies in Higher Education, Berkeley, California. Some minor details of classification omitted.)

The numbers used in the classification will not transfer to the British scene, but, broadly, all our universities would qualify as 'doctorate-granting', and most polytechnics as at least seeking to be so; while a number of higher education colleges, formed from teacher training colleges, would fall in class 5 or 6. But, just as we lack institutions with two-year programmes, so we are also very light in institutions which extend *only* to a first degree, or *only* to a Master's degree, and are relatively very heavily committed to institutions with the full range, including doctoral programmes. Substantial inequality in the receipt of research funds exists in Britain, as in the United States, though the incautious should be warned that the figures can be distorted by the accident of involvement in 'heavy science'. But all universities and polytechnics, together with a number of other institutions, regard themselves as having some research interest, and there is considerable pressure to spread research funds more widely.

Should we seek, by the year 2000, to have a greater differentiation? Among the universities, thinking has not been very friendly to the idea that excellence resides in an institution, rather than in its separate subject departments. Oxford and Cambridge do indeed tend to regard themselves as excellent, but, though they enjoy a high standard of academic living, there are many subjects for which neither Oxford nor Cambridge would be a first choice for study or research. On the other hand, I can call to mind no university, however recent or small or remote, which cannot properly claim to be in the lead in some area of its work. It might seem, therefore, that a policy of diffused excellence, with no clear differentiation, has worked rather well, each of the equal universities being allowed a chance to excel in something.

But there are two weaknesses in this argument. The same 'parity of esteem' is sought by thirty polytechnics, and few people have been able to imagine British higher education as having at the top a class of over seventy institutions, all placed 'equal first'. An even greater weakness appears if we examine the obverse of the assertion that each university is excellent in something. Each university (and each polytechnic) is bad, inadequate, old-fashioned, pedestrian or perverse in some, and perhaps in many, of its subject areas. Yet each seeks (now or for the future) to develop research, to attract funds, and to provide doctoral programmes over almost the whole range of its activities, good and bad. Lack of differentiation implies pressure to fund inadequate research, in order to be 'fair'; it implies that Ph.D.s are being given in departments so inadequate or badly funded that they offer no valid inspiration or experience.

I conclude that it is necessary to grasp the nettle of differentiation, and to use, between now and the year 2000, the persuasive instruments of research funding and studentship allocation to achieve it. I have already suggested that some colleges should meet the need for two-year courses. Others should be concerned with lower level or undergraduate courses only, recruiting staff as teachers, and not expecting research as a main objective. Others – and this group might include a majority of the polytechnics and some of the existing universities – should not claim competence to teach beyond the level of a Master's degree, and they too should regard teaching as a more important commitment of staff than research; they might expect a three-to-one division of effort, rather than the common assumption of one-to-one. (It is, of course, an implication of this that the luxurious staff-student ratios now common would no longer be permitted, but would worsen, perhaps to the point found appropriate in some of the better American universities and colleges). Those institutions claiming to be major centres of research, and therefore proper places for training doctoral candidates, should not make this claim over the whole range of their activities. There should be no more than about a dozen major research centres for any subject – and fewer, perhaps only two, for minority subjects; these research centres, with their associated doctoral programmes, would be distributed, not equally, over perhaps thirty to thirty-five institutions.

In Chapter 8 I suggest that it is scholarship, rather than research in the sense of establishing new knowledge, which is the essential ingredient in enlivening teaching and giving it authority. I do not therefore see the suggested concentration of research as producing thirty or thirty-five good teaching institutions, and a lot of indifferent ones. On the contrary: those who give more time and thought to teaching, provided they have broad knowledge of their subject and a lively interest in its development, are likely to be the better teachers. There is an essential provision for the maintenance of scholarship – freedom to travel to meet other scholars, and to use major libraries – and this provision will be needed in all the types of institution.

Obviously a change to a differentiated system would be very unpopular, for even those who have argued for special recognition of excellence usually begin from the assumption that the excellence of their own university or department is self-evident. The change would bring into the open what already exists, a difference between institutions in the intellectual quality of undergraduates recruited. But the case for mixed ability classes in higher education has never really been studied, still less proved. I think it likely that there would be benefit from a greater degree of 'streaming', both for the intellectually brilliant, who would have to test themselves in a competitive and demanding environment, and for the more pedestrian, who would tend to go to places with a stronger commitment to teaching and a fuller appreciation of the best methods to use.

There is no need, however, to present the change as a downgrading of some colleges, for new opportunities would exist, and these might be more exciting than seeking to be an imperfect copy of Oxford or Manchester University. The lesson to be learnt from the Open University is that there has been a large unsatisfied demand for higher education courses among older students. The Open University concerns itself mainly with those who are willing in principle to take a complete degree, and it rations its admissions; the likelihood is, therefore, that many other students would be interested in a more flexible and open scheme. And there is a demand for newly-designed courses for mature students at a lower level, as the 'Open College' scheme in the North-West has demonstrated. The methods of the Open University are not the only way of providing for the needs of mature students; some find themselves able to take normal full-time courses, others would be attracted by evening courses or by 'summer semesters' of the American type, and others by short periods of full-time study with intermediate periods of supervised home learning.

The enthusiasts in this area seem to expect almost everyone to 'go back to school' at frequent intervals to update knowledge and gain new intellectual enrichment. Such an expectation underestimates the economic and practical difficulties, and overestimates the place of institutional learning in the education which is given by the whole of life. Nevertheless, the demand for higher-level courses is likely to go on increasing, and the idea of a flexible programme of education, not all concentrated in a few early years, will become more popular; some changes in methods of student finance would facilitate this flexibility (see p. 115). The institutions in a diversified system which have a primary commitment to teaching could do much to provide for the demand from mature students.

They could also have a special role in relation to the under-privileged. In the United States, universities and colleges are expected, and sometimes required, to give special attention to underprivileged groups by acts of 'positive discrimination' or by what is technically known as 'affirmative action'. But this, by itself, may fail to get to the root of the matter. Few of the underprivileged are excluded by prejudice; most are held back by the cumulative influence of their background and associations throughout the years of education. The problem of providing opportunity for West Indians, or even for women, is not essentially different from that of providing it for the children of unskilled labourers. The task, by the time the age for higher education is attained, is to kindle ambition and remedy deficiencies. A great deal remains to be done in this area, both in finding the right approach and in devising efficient forms of remedial action. Even though the main burden of putting right the deficiencies of background must rest elsewhere (p. 30), the institutions with a teaching priority could do much more to help. The social conscience of the academic community has been sadly unawakened on this matter.

Another group deserving special consideration is that of the overseas students. British higher education has a reputation which makes it highly attractive to students from many parts of the world. Some have the ability and the cultural background to fit easily into the normal processes of British universities and colleges. Many more need special attention if they are to find their full potential, and many fail to get this attention. The problem is more than language, though this is often important: the foundation laid by school studies may be so different that the student lacks information or ideas which his British fellows are assumed to possess. If some of our colleges would make a speciality of assessing the problems of students from a particular area of the world, and providing systematically for their correction *before* the plunge into a normal higher education course is taken, the value of higher education as an export industry and as a means of giving us a world-wide group of friends could be greatly increased.

The broad conclusion of this chapter is that the institutions of the year 2000, while not rigidly planned, should be encouraged to develop more variety than those we have at present. At one side would be the great centres of research and higher learning, more concentrated in their activities, and serving the whole country and the world. At the other would be colleges which would open new possibilities of general and vocational education to the less ambitious products of the 'new' sixth forms, and their equivalents in tertiary colleges and elsewhere. Between would be a range of teaching institutions, expert in their task, to provide undergraduate and masters' degree courses and to make a special contribution in helping the educationally underprivileged and the overseas student. The majority of all these institutions would have their main interests in the locality or the region rather the whole country, and this would help them to seek out opportunities of serving a local community as a base for general adult education, a source for information and advice, and a means of providing limited research help. We are in some danger of getting too many nationally-orientated bodies, and of falling into the bad habit of regarding a local interest as implying a limited or parochial attitude. A diversification which encouraged local roots would therefore be timely.

The proposal for diversification is open to attack on the grounds of inconsistency with what I have earlier said about planning and its dangers. One is tempted to have recourse to Emerson's remark, that 'A foolish consistency is the hobgoblin of little minds.... Speak what you think today in words as hard as cannon-balls, and tomorrow speak what tomorrow thinks in hard words again, though it contradict every thing you said today'. But there is no need for such excuses, for the inconsistency is only apparent. The doubts about planning relate to attempts to regulate in detail what each institution should do. But the freedom with which I contrast a planned system is not unconstrained; it provides a variety of response within the broad guiding influence of the systems of finance. Those systems at present spread research funds widely, support graduate courses at many centres, finance degree studies with more certainty than is available for sub-degree studies. By doing so they determine some of the features of British higher education which I have criticized. What I seek is an alteration of the guiding influences, and the establishment of a new variety of response to the new circumstances. There would of course be hard choices to be made – which dozen physics departments should be major centres of research, and how does one make changes in the list, so as to ensure that no selected centre could relapse into somnolence? Such choices would require wise advisers, but they do not call for more wisdom than existing choices which affect the shape of the system, such as that about the balance of finance between the universities and the public sector. What a differentiated system does need, however, is bravery by decision-makers; it is much easier to pretend that everyone has an equal claim to everything than to admit an intention to create differences.

A NOTE ABOUT OXFORD AND CAMBRIDGE
The universities of Oxford and Cambridge are widely regarded throughout the world (and not least in Oxford and Cambridge) as the summit of the British higher education system. They are collegiate universities, like Durham, Kent, York and Lancaster, and they have the special feature that in both, and especially in Oxford, the colleges have substantial teaching functions. Students are admitted by colleges, and not by the university; general tutorial care and academic advice is given by the colleges; and the colleges provide or regulate the living accommodation of the students, and offer a centre for their social life. The colleges are private charitable foundations, receiving no direct state aid, but subsisting on their endowments and on the fees obtained from students.

The universities also have substantial endowments, and they differ in many respects from the rest of the university system. They are in practice controlled by the academic staff of the university and colleges. The systems of payment are very complex, but generally yield substantially higher incomes to those below the rank of professor than they would obtain elsewhere. Those members of staff who are Fellows of colleges enjoy privileges such as dining rights, rooms or sets of rooms, and a variety of services. Despite the possession of endowments, the university and college together levy substantially higher fees than are payable at other universities. The grants made by the UGC take only partial account of the total endowments, so that the amount spent per student is high; and although a part of this spending is accounted for by the high cost of maintaining ancient buildings, which is a contribution to the national heritage, there is no doubt whatever that the 'standard of academic living' is high, with a multitude of facilities and advantages both for students and staff which are the envy of the rest of the higher education system.

This higher spending could be fully justified if Oxford and Cambridge were seen to have a particular function in higher education, to provide some defined and costly special excellence, or perhaps to specialize in higher degree work. But, great as is the distinction of both universities in particular departments, that distinction is patchy, and there are subject-areas criticized for inefficient and neglectful teaching, particularly of graduate students, and subject-areas where an apparently lavish provision of resources does not establish intellectual leadership. Furthermore, although both universities recruit first degree students of high achievement at school, they actually receive fewer applications than other universities, and a much higher proportion of their recruitment is from the 'public' (that is, private) schools outside the state system. This means that Oxford and Cambridge are recruiting, to a disproportionate extent, from well-to-do professional and managerial class families. The children of such families enjoy an educational advantage from an early age, and their high performance at school may yield an overestimate of the abilities which they will show in later life.

There is a strong bias towards the 'upper' socio-economic classes in most of higher education, and this is rightly regarded with concern. It cannot, therefore, be a matter of indifference that these two prestigious universities show the bias to an exceptional degree, and – through the excellence of their connections with particular forms of employment – transfer it to key areas in the economic and social system.

If Oxford and Cambridge are doing a job of teaching and research not essentially different from that performed by, say, the Universities of London and Edinburgh, then there is no justification for levying higher fees than elsewhere, and indeed the endowments might well be held to imply that fees should be lower. If Oxford and Cambridge are doing a special job, justifying some unusual degree of academic luxury, then that job needs to be much more clearly defined than it is at present. In either case, those habits and practices which lead to a recruitment even more narrow in its social base than that of other universities should be changed.

The graduates of Oxford and Cambridge occupy very many of the key positions in the Establishment, and this is no doubt why the anomalous position of the two universities continues with little question or debate; both have many friends who regard it as self-evident that Oxford and Cambridge should get special treatment, though they might find it difficult to explain why. It is time that the issues were properly explored by an appropriately independent Commission. It may well be that a special function for the two universities could be a most valuable feature of the British higher education system; but that function remains to be discovered.

6
THE CURRICULUM

What matters about a university or college is the detail of its everyday activity. So much is obvious; and yet there is often a tendency to discuss the future of higher education in terms of numbers, costs, systems and organizations, with little reference to what the entities being discussed actually do. Fifteen of the hundred and seventy-eight recommendations of the Robbins Committee related to university courses, and a scatter of others to courses elsewhere in the higher education system; but the list includes obvious generalities such as that 'students who do not live up to their early promise should be transferred, after their first or second year, to less exacting courses.' The recommendations about the substance of the curriculum number about five, the most important being those encouraging 'broader' courses. The vast output of the Carnegie Commission in the United States was about almost everything except the curriculum, though, of course, the expressions of view on the purposes of higher education had evident curricular implications. Happily, however, the balance has been set right by the Carnegie Council on Policy Studies in Higher Education and by the Carnegie Foundation for the Advancement of Teaching, which commissioned between them three studies of the purposes, history and current facts of the undergraduate curriculum in American colleges and universities. One of these is prefaced by an anonymous remark which represents the puzzlement of academic man in face of the vast complexity of the curricular offerings accumulated over the years, and provides an appropriate starting point for this discussion:

The curriculum does not matter. If it did matter, we could not do

anything about it. If we could do something about it, we would
not know what to do.

Those who say that the curriculum does not matter mean,
I think, that the essence of higher education is in the quality
of the relationship of master to scholar. Given good teachers,
'alive with living thoughts' (in Whitehead's words), good
consequences will follow. Such an argument comes dangerously close to an assertion that only method matters, and not
content. The content of what is taught is surely the principal
expression of the excellence of the teachers. If the curriculum is
ill-adapted to the educational needs of students, it is time for the
teachers to be challenged to look at the quality of their work.

But no-one with experience in this field will lack sympathy
for the plea 'we could not do anything about it'. The curriculum
of a university or college is a complex interlocking structure.
For the Cambridge Tripos examinations, a student may study
entirely within the bounds of a single faculty, but this degree
of specialization is rare even in intentionally specialized degrees.
More usually a student follows courses from a range of departments, and in the broader degrees which Robbins favoured
that range may be a wide one, crossing the traditional boundaries of faculties. The alteration of a curriculum tends, therefore,
to need the consent of a large number of people. In some
instances that consent must be given by bodies outside the
university or college, for instance professional associations
which set minimum requirements. But the larger the numbers
involved in the decision, the less likely it becomes that there
will be a consensus about the purposes of what is being attempted. It becomes relatively easy to block any proposal
which involves excisions from an existing curriculum, and
change tends to be confined to additions, which further compli-
cate the structure, until only a few experts know about it and
can remember the justification for its parts.

What this amounts to is that by far the most important
determinant of a curriculum is its own past history. It preserves,
like fossils, the ideas of yesterday, while still adding the sediment

of today's ideas. The curricula of higher education differ greatly from one country to another, but there is no ready way of identifying one type as generally 'best', for what appears good in one country would not rest satisfactorily on the historical accretions of another. Waves of discontent with the curriculum occur in many countries – an example was the student pressure, in the late 1960s and early 1970s, for more 'relevance' – but the structure remains resistant to change. The files of higher education contain many reports of committees which have proposed brave curricular innovations, only to find the essence of their proposals ignored.

In 1937 and 1938, however, St. John's College in Annapolis scrapped the whole of its existing curriculum in favour of a prescribed four-year course for all students based on about a hundred Great Books covering the development of civilization from ancient Greece to the present day. Every student attends seminars to discuss readings in the books, and also laboratory classes and group tutorials in language, mathematics and music. This celebrated example, a more extreme reform than that achieved at the University of Chicago, suggests that a break with past history is not totally impossible. But St. John's was virtually bankrupt, it had just fired its president, allegedly for the improper grant of a degree, it had lost its 'accreditation' (that is, academic recognition), and was fast losing its students. This put the incoming president and dean in an unassailable position to dictate. No British institution is likely to have such an opportunity.

Yet we must not give up hope. Ideas are powerful, and the conventional wisdom of the past sometimes collapses in a surprising way. If higher education is to achieve its purposes, substantial changes of content will certainly be needed before the year 2000. Let us consider what those changes should be.

First, I pick up from Chapters 2 and 3 what is there said about the requirements of society and of the individual:

A supply of people with a range of skills and an extent of understanding which will make them capable both of

*rapid learning of an initial task and of subsequent adap-
tation to changing demands; the 'extent of understanding'
implying* both *an appreciation of basic principles, scientific laws or statistical associations in the main field of
interest,* and *a sufficient appreciation of related fields.*

*The enrichment of culture: an advanced knowledge of a part
of our heritage which can be a basis for new achievement.*

A high state of understanding of the workings of society.

*A critical and questioning mind which initiates change where
change is appropriate.*

The development of higher-level cognitive skills.

Deeper understanding of ethical problems.

*The attainment of emotional maturity and balance, and the
learning of social skills.*

The development of creative skills and aesthetic appreciation.

Not all of this range of requirements needs to find a place in
a formal curriculum; some elements may belong better to the
informal influence of the corporate life of the institution.
What is needed by a particular individual is affected by what the
school, the family and society in general have given him or
her in earlier years; by what can properly be left to the training
programmes of employers or to the influence of the workplace;
and by what is offered by general educational influences – the
press, the television and radio, the paper-back book – during
the period of higher education. And what can be given to an
individual depends, not just on his needs, but on certain hard
facts about what can be done within a given time. Breadth can
generally only be achieved at a loss in depth of study of a
main field. If an employer is saying 'You will only be recognized
as qualified if you have covered these and these subjects',
it may be necessary to leave out other important things in
order to satisfy the vocational urge of the student.

Since there is no time to do everything, where do we look
for the essentials? Any advanced study will require some basic
knowledge of materials, facts and methods. The successful

medical student must know the essential facts of human anatomy. The mathematician must master the methods of differentiation and integration, and know how to solve certain equations and to sum certain series. The economist would (I hope) be regarded as ill-educated if he had never read a word of Keynes. Some teachers in higher education treat a whole course as a body of material to be mastered, with no requirement to know anything outside what is directly taught, and no expectation that the student will have any thoughts other than those he has copied down from his teacher or his prescribed books. But this would generally be thought bad education: the emphasis goes the other way, towards minimising 'rote learning' and encouraging independent thought and a free range of study. Facts can be looked up in reference books when they are needed; methods can be reproduced from worked examples. It is a mistake, however, to attempt to reduce the basic core of fact, method and prescribed material too much. It would be difficult to imagine fruitful communication between economists, for instance, if it was not possible to assume a common knowledge of the elements of Keynesian employment theory.

But there is an awkward zone of uncertainty between the knowledge which is basic and essential and that which is merely desirable. It is *desirable* that an economist should be widely read in economic history, sociology, social psychology, politics, economic geography, management, accounting, operational research, systems theory and other subjects; in practice he plainly cannot be, at least during his initial studies in higher education. It is here that we confront one of the choices which relate to depth and breadth (or to 'specialization' and 'general courses'). The student who spends most of his time within the confines of a single discipline can exercise his mind on more difficult material, but he loses the opportunities of insight which often come at the crossing-points between one discipline and another. At the extreme, he is in danger of becoming the sort of desiccated specialist who is quite incapable of imagining that any discipline but his own can be relevant to the problems he meets in his work or his life. On the other hand, the student who spends his time on a related set of subjects – normally having a central interest, but studying other subjects which illuminate that interest – is in danger of becoming superficial, 'Jack of all trades and master of none'.

The type of breadth just discussed, which can be called 'looking over the wall', can be distinguished from another, 'looking far away'. This is the exposure of the student to subjects quite different from his main interest; the purpose being to give an understanding of the methods and content of other disciplines, and to develop a broader culture. Such an exposure can either be a required feature of the curriculum, or it can be the free choice of the student, who is allowed to select courses from a wide range. The idea of achieving this type of breadth became prominent as a consequence of the 'Two Cultures' discussion – that is, the exposure of the dangers which arise from lack of common understanding between scientists and non-scientists. In fact, of course, there are not two cultures but many, merging into each other, but having a range such that divisions other than that between the scientist and the rest can be significant; both the physicist and the historian may be quite at a loss in the culture of the artist. There is also a barrier to understanding between scientists and engineers, and this may be particularly damaging because many people imagine engineering to be a branch of science.

It is not obvious, of course, that sampling a very different discipline is an effective way of producing imaginative understanding of it. If the breadth of study is imposed, it may be ineffective because courses make little mark on the unwilling student; if it is attained by the free choice of the student, it may be so random that it fails to deal effectively with the important cultural divisions. The progress which can be made, in a lesser part of the time of study, in understanding a subject for which no preparation has been made may be so small as not to be worth having. Certainly there seems to be little point in simply allowing students from another discipline to take courses designed for a particular specialism. A science course which is to do a good job in enlightening the arts student about scientific method needs to be specially designed with that in mind; and the same is true for a course intended to help scientists to have a fuller sense of the potentialities of language, or one to encourage economists to understand what artists are seeking to do.

The curricula actually available in the year 2000 will no doubt be very various; but can we foresee any general direction of movement on this question of specialization and breadth? Over the last twenty years there has been some shift away from extremes of specialization in the schools, and a notable increase in the number of students who do not fit into the compartments of 'arts', 'science' and 'social science', but have taken, right to the A-level stage, subjects from two or even three of these sections. As far as can be seen, the movement towards reduced specialization is continuing, though this is an uncertain prediction, since it is probable that proposals to reform the A-level examinations in a way which encourages breadth will be defeated by the rising power of those who are worried about the levels of attainment achieved in school. However, enough change has already occurred to suggest that more time may be needed for specialization in higher education, rather than less, and that the need to encourage the crossing of cultural lines may be less than it was.

This suggests a curriculum which has, for each student, a strong specialist core, with the associated necessary basic studies, for example mathematics for physicists, and with any remaining time being used for studying *related* subjects, 'looking over the wall'. The optimum curriculum might therefore be somewhat like that which was common in the large 'civic' universities twenty years ago, and new-fangled experiments in the 'new' universities and some of the polytechnics would no longer be in fashion.

This rather depressing conclusion would however imply that the informal experiences of living are adequate to carry all the functions of education beyond the development of cognitive skills and the provision of useful workers to the economy. Such a view needs to be challenged, and a further discussion can conveniently start by looking at an attractively Utopian idea. Patricia Cross (*Accent on Learning*, San Francisco: Jossey-Bass, 1976) proposes a curriculum with three elements – working with ideas, working with people, and working with things – in which the requirement for graduation would be excellence in one area and adequacy in the other two. Apart from teaching some skills with 'things' to artists, engineers and scientists, and skills with 'people' to social workers and perhaps to doctors and psychologists, most of higher education is concerned with ideas; so this would be a change indeed. The university of Newman, wholly concerned with intellectual matters, would give way to an institution concerned with the full range of individual development, in which the craftsman and the peacemaker would be honoured equally with the mathematician or historian.

Several arguments against such a change could be developed. The least credible of these are those which assert some sort of primacy of esteem for the intellectual. It was a habit, when I was an undergraduate reading mathematics, to look down on engineering as a subject 'smelling of the workshop', never capable of reaching the sublime intellectual heights of the Queen of the Sciences. This was dangerous snobbery; no necessary part of human endeavour should be regarded as a second-class activity. A rather more credible argument is that suggested above, that the understanding of personal relationships and of the handling of 'things' is best developed informally and voluntarily, outside any set curriculum. Many people, for instance, develop unexpected qualities of craftsmanship when they have a home or a garden to look after. Alternatively, it can be argued that the development of skills with 'things' can be adequately completed at school, and that the growth of skills with people is necessarily a slow one, not capable of being contained in a curriculum, but arising from exposure to the varied experiences of life.

But these arguments may be more convenient than valid. Graduates from higher education are plainly not always well-rounded in their development. The list of student priorities on

p. 32 suggests that there is dissatisfaction with this situation; that the argument that 'you can learn these skills for yourselves' is not found fully convincing. I would myself wish to take two things from Patricia Cross's proposals, though they are at different levels of urgency.

The lesser of these is that craftsmanship, design, manual and athletic skill, and the practice of music, drama and the fine arts should be seen to have a higher place on the agenda of universities. (They are often better served by the non-university colleges, though, even there, more could be done.) This is partly a matter of being seen not to accept a false class distinction. So far as time allows, one would wish to see such subjects develop, not just as specialisms for students with a vocational intent, but as means of fuller development for students of other subjects. I would put particular stress on helping students to think about what is beautiful and worth preserving, for many seem to have no ability to look at and listen to the world around them and divide what is good from what is ugly or transitory.

The major point, however, relates to skills with people. The division between 'working with ideas' and 'working with people' is not a hard one. Practice in personal relationships is very important, and must indeed be largely obtained by exposure to the accidents of life, but it is possible to prepare for that practice through the intellect, that is, by encouraging deeper and more systematic thought on the problems likely to arise. These are often problems of morals and ethics: Why be unselfish? Why be truthful? When does a greater good justify the doing of an apparent evil? The serious consideration of dilemmas in personal relationships cannot be left entirely to the schools, since a reasonable maturity is needed to appreciate the issues. There is thus a case for providing within the higher education curriculum for the serious study of relationships.

But this is difficult. British higher education is no longer built on religious foundations, and, though its teachers no doubt convey something of their attitude to life, the explicit discussion of moral dilemmas as part of the programme of teaching is rare, and the evangelistic enthusiasm for particular ways of resolving them is mostly left to the committed members of the extreme political Left. It is, of course, perfectly possible to help people to understand a problem without demanding their assent to a particular solution, but it is easier to dodge the issues. This evasion affects, not only preparation for personal relationships, but also, in some degree, preparation for citizenship and political life, for here too there are issues which involve moral dilemmas – for instance, what is the proper place of force, coercion, punishment? What is the right extent of inequality? What weight should be given to harm done to future generations by the satisfaction of present needs? The reply of higher education institutions on such matters can be caricatured as 'We would rather not discuss the matter, but if you must have a view, we have a proper academic neutrality between good and evil.' The great issues of life are discussed, if at all, at a low intellectual level; and this may be one reason why students complain of a lack of 'relevance'.

The problem to which this points is that discussed by Sir Walter Moberly more than thirty years ago (*The Crisis in the University*, London: SCM Press, 1949):

Our predicament then is this. Most students go through our universities without ever having been forced to exercise their minds on the issues which are really momentous ... Owing to the prevailing fragmentation of studies, they are not challenged to decide responsibly on a life-purpose or equipped to make such a decision wisely. They are not incited to disentangle and examine critically the assumptions and emotional attitudes underlying the particular studies they pursue, the profession for which they are preparing, the ethical judgements they are accustomed to make, and the political or religious convictions they hold. Fundamentally they are uneducated.

Such a complaint lies mainly against the character of teachers, and alleges a *trahison des clercs*; but it suggests that the teachers in higher education ought to be challenged to include, at least among the options of their curricula, courses which lead students to think more deeply about some of the dilemmas of personal, social and political life. The point of entry might well be to take dilemmas which relate to the student's main field of interest. Thus, the biologist might be encouraged to think of the contradictions which arise from a desire to protect wild life, and the economist of the implications of the fact that perpetual economic growth is impossible. But – returning to Patricia Cross's proposal – there would certainly be takers also for courses which lead to deeper thought on problems of personal life.

The curriculum which we look for in the year 2000 might thus contain four elements:

1 *The specialist core and the associated basic studies.*

2 *The related subject or subjects.*

3 *The examination of some implications of the specialist studies.*

4 *An optional course, which might be used for the study of other dilemmas of personal, social or political life, or for acquiring a deeper aesthetic appreciation, or in other ways (so far as time allows) for cultural broadening.*

This is not an ideal curriculum, if we were free from the hard limitations of time. People will in future have more leisure, and it could well be argued that they need a more systematic preparation to use it constructively; this would imply a broad range of studies in addition to any specialist preparation for work. Many commentators have pointed to the need for flexibility which arises from rapid technological change; this flexibility also suggests a widening of the range of studies, with an emphasis throughout on principles rather than on specific techniques. But we must be realistic. A general lengthening of the period of higher education is not a likely priority for social expenditure in Britain during the next twenty years, though some lengthening of particular courses, for example in engineering, may well occur. A full provision for cultural breadth and for flexibility would, in these circumstances, altogether squeeze out the discipline of going into a subject fully and deeply. It would be highly dangerous to our future as an advanced nation to avoid the intellectual rigour provided by a hard core of specialist studies. Hence it will be necessary to lean more heavily on the various forms of adult education, on the training provided by employers, and on the informal influences of literature, radio and television, to provide the extra breadth and flexibility which cannot be contained in an initial course.

Three questions now arise. To what extent should student choice be allowed or encouraged within this curriculum? Is the general pattern appropriate to shorter or lower-level courses, for instance in the proposed junior colleges, as well as to undergraduate degree courses? How does the pattern set out above relate to the work done at the postgraduate level?

The value of allowing a wide choice is that, hopefully, a better level of motivation is achieved. If a lot of time can be allowed, students can be permitted to roam quite widely while still covering the essential basic elements. There is, however, a serious disadvantage, namely that if those who take course A are not *required* to take course B there is a reason, or excuse, to plan the two courses quite separately, and to give no attention to the ways in which they might support or illuminate each other. This is particularly unfortunate if it breaks the link between the 'main' and the 'related' subjects, because it is here that interaction is most desirable. Furthermore, within the short period of a British degree, or similar course, there is really not enough time to allow an extensive choice, while still covering what is essential. I once served in a university where a possible option was to take Hebrew, economics and astronomy, but I remain unconvinced that the freedom to do so was worth defending.

I would therefore suggest a scheme like this, as applicable to many subjects:

COMPULSORY	LIMITED CHOICE
Essentials of main subject with associated basic studies	*Branches of main subject (to be studied late in course)*
Related subject or subjects	
Implications of main subject.	*Option of type 4 above.*

The reader will note that this leaves unanswered the question 'what is a subject?' To this I return shortly.

Is the same pattern appropriate to shorter courses? I believe that it is. I note in particular that there is a semantic confusion about 'general education', which ought to mean 'general development of the mind and ability, not related to a specific vocation'. General education does not have to be 'general' in the sense of being served on an hors d'oeuvre dish, for the student to sample little bits of many things. On the contrary; the shorter the course, the more attention needs to be given to achieving significant progress in a specific area. If the assumption of a gradual broadening of school education is correct, then junior college courses as well as degree courses can afford to attempt some depth of study in a particular area.

The position of higher degree studies is confused. For some years now, emphasis has been placed on the 'taught course', for an M.A. or equivalent degree; that is, on an extension into more advanced areas of specialization than can be accommodated in the undergraduate course. Although such courses may be taken out of pure curiosity and a desire for greater cultural depth, most students who take them have a vocational reason. Some, however, will drift into Masters' degree courses because they are unwilling to face the world of work, and it will therefore be wise to give special encouragement to courses intended for those returning to academic study after some years of work. The other side of the encouragement of taught courses has been a generally frosty attitude towards 'research' degrees. These are regarded by employers as over-developed, and as being very often the refuge of weak characters who are unwilling to depart from the familiar surroundings of a university.

In fact, however, the research or Ph.D. degree serves two different purposes. In some subjects, and notably in the sciences, it is a certificate of research training. It commonly certifies that a student has become familiar with the processes of a laboratory, that he has worked acceptably and usefully as part of a team, and that he has shown an adequate ability in explaining his own contribution to discovery by that team. The element of originality is sometimes slight, and the pretence of independence largely eyewash; but at least the successful candidate can be recommended to the world as suitably trained for a job in research. There is plainly a function for such training, but it is essentially vocational, and the provision made for it need not exceed the demands of employers for run-of-the-mill, competent researchers. Of course, employers would like their research staff to be not just competent, but brilliant, original and acutely practical; some of their disappointment may arise from the natural fact that such special people are in short supply.

But there are also research degrees, common in the arts and social science subjects, in which the emphasis on independence and originality is much stronger. Indeed, the candidate is often left largely to himself to find out facts and develop ideas, with only occasional help from his supervisor, and it is a proper criticism of some such degrees that no real provision is made for research training. Some departments, indeed, seem to regard time spent with research students as a mere fringe activity. One problem with these degrees is to find a worthwhile subject, and it is easy to point the finger of scorn at someone who 'knows more and more about less and less', and whose claim to academic distinction is that he or she is the only person in the whole world to have studied some minor Catalan poet whose works deserve total oblivion. But those who can succeed in making an original contribution on a significant subject are surely among the most valuable products of higher education, the very stuff of which both economic success and cultural vigour are made.

It is interesting to note that experiments in 'independent studies' at undergraduate level, by which each student follows a course specially devised for his needs and commonly involving a large element of private study, go some way to develop the same qualities. An original contribution to knowledge is not to be expected at undergraduate level, though it is occasionally obtained; but the attempt at a private intellectual adventure can, if it comes off, have most valuable results. Schemes of 'independent studies' are too costly in supervisory time to be generally adopted, and in any case they appear to attract only a minority of students, mostly mature. For this special group, they deserve to flourish.

I thus see the place of higher degrees in the curriculum as involving three elements:

1 Taught courses in advanced areas of specialization; most commonly taken for a vocational reason, which includes, of course, training the next generation of teachers in higher education, and likely in that case to be most effectively used if chosen deliberately after a period of work experience.

2 Training for a career which includes research; which should be seen as a vocational demand, and could be planned more effectively than at present.

3 Provision for the development of intellectual adventure on a worth-while subject. This should be encouraged and generously supported, but within the limits that high standards of importance of the subject and of originality of the outcome should be set.

These are not alternative courses – some students may pass through all three. They omit what is occasionally seen as a bad habit, the conferring of a higher degree for work which is essentially no different to that done in a first degree. Provision should certainly be made for taking an additional first degree in shortened time, but it is misleading to give it a postgraduate title.

I have expressed some approval, in the particular circumstances of Britain in the year 2000, of specialization in a subject;

but what is a subject? Ought we to be satisfied with the traditional boundaries of academic subjects? What is the place of 'joint' courses involving two or more main subjects? What provision should we make for new subjects to enter the curriculum, for old ones to leave it, and for boundaries to be redefined?

There is no authority which defines subjects; they are in fact sociologically determined, as the work of groups of scholars who consort together out of a common interest in an area. Some of these groups are highly stable, and relate to well-defined professions with a particular place in the structure of society, like lawyers. Others have episodes of fission and recombination; thus there has in recent years been some tendency for botanists, zoologists, geneticists and the like to think of themselves as 'biologists', and to resent any suggestion that the subject is sub-divided. Some subject-groups are minor cells within a larger organism (like mediaeval French within French studies), and some migrate from one larger grouping to another; thus, the economic historians have had difficulty in deciding whether they are 'predominantly' historians, or 'predominantly' economists, or would work better as an independent group, using the techniques of history and ecnomics but not absorbed by either.

New subjects appear in the curriculum for a variety of reasons:

1 Sometimes the demands of a growing profession for a higher quality of intake and for research on its problems leads to the establishment of new groups of scholars. The appearance of marketing and operational research as distinct subjects provide examples. But this is a difficult birth-process, which depends on the existence of a small number of scholars in other disciplines, or practitioners of the new subject with an academic bent, who can provide the nucleus for the new group. Subjects created in this way tend for a long time to be thought academically inferior, unless they can borrow respectability from a parent subject (as operational research can, from mathematics).

2 Sometimes a group which has provided a minor special-ism within some other subject becomes so popular that it attains independent status by fission. Thus in universities accounting was once weakly represented, generally as a sub-sidiary subject taught by one or two staff in economics or commerce departments; in the further education colleges it existed mainly as an aid to study for professional examinations, sometimes taught by part-time staff and sometimes taken mainly by part-time students. The recent overwhelming popu-larity of the subject has produced large departments of full-time staff, teaching full-time students for specialist accounting degrees. This process of fission has greatly increased the cohes-ion of accounting staff and their potential contribution in research.

3 Sometimes the development of knowledge makes it inevitable that a group of scholars will seek independent status. Thus the rapid developments in linguistics have established the subject as a major area of study in its own right, which plainly cannot rest in any one language department.

4 Occasionally someone makes a deliberate effort to fill in a blank space in the map of knowledge, by inviting ap-propriate scholars to come and study in a new area. But this also is a difficult process; the 'new' subjects tend to be new names for old activities, and genuine social cohesion round a deliberately chosen new point is not easily achieved.

All this adds up to a menu of subjects which changes oc-casionally, but not very much. Its chief fault is that, whereas some subject-groups have formed around *things*, others have formed around *methods* or *attitudes*. Biology covers all forms of study of living things. Economics, however, does not cover all forms of study of the activities of producing, consuming, buying and selling, despite Marshall's definition of it as 'a study of mankind in the ordinary business of life'; for sig-nificant aspects of behaviour in this area need the contribution of sociology and social psychology. A statistics department is mainly about methods. Even an English literature depart-ment, though it appears to be about a 'thing' – the corpus of

English literature – is in practice circumscribed by its methods or habits of study and criticism. It will commonly, for instance, fail to illuminate to the full the historical and social background of the times in which or about which the literature was written – for this is the province of the historian and the sociologist.

Dedicated scholars often appear not to mind wearing blinkers. The fascination of their subject is enough reward, even if it touches only lightly on the reality it purports to study. Many economists have written learned papers on banking, without ever confusing themselves by talking to a banker to find out what he actually does. The average student, however, is more likely to be well-motivated if he feels that he is looking at a problem 'in the round'. Hence there is a good deal of impatience with the traditional boundaries of subjects, and some desire to see things more broadly by taking combinations of subjects: economics with sociology, accounting with economics, English with history, politics with history, and so on. The calendars of universities and colleges are full of joint degrees with all sorts of combinations of subjects.

There is a different case for joint courses to provide a professional qualification in two subjects; for instance, those intending to teach languages do well to be able to offer two foreign languages, not one. Apart from this, however, experience suggests that the attempt to achieve a more rounded approach by taking two *equal* subjects (which is something different from having a major specialization with minor subsidiaries) is not very successful, and indeed many of the combinations offered are seldom taken. This is again because of the limitations of time: a satisfying degree of penetration of the interests of two different groups of scholars cannot be achieved, and students vote with their feet in favour of deeper specialization in one area, even though they may remain dissatisfied with the limitations of view so imposed.

Yet, if we look at the matter more deeply, the trouble is that each subject-department has a rigid idea of what a good student ought to know, and the joint courses are simply adding together the menu items prescribed by each. A student of English can perhaps be let off Chaucer, but he must, in many institutions, study Shakespeare, eighteenth-century literature, nineteenth-century literature, and modern literature. A historian has to be selective, from the world-wide scope and the many centuries available, but history courses will generally cover a considerable range. Yet a satisfying degree of depth and interaction might well be obtained by, say, a course on life and culture in eighteenth-century England, which would concentrate on the literature, art and manner of living of that period, relating it to historical events and to what needs to be known about preceding centuries and other countries, but not attempting to produce a professional English scholar or a professional historian of the normal range.

This sort of new course, using a variety of *methods* and *approaches* to study a particular 'thing', ought to become much more common by the year 2000. It can combine some of the virtues of specialization with those of 'breadth' and interaction. The reason why such courses are not more frequent is that they are hard work, and cannot be achieved by simply adding together what is provided for specialist English scholars and specialist historians. It would be good to see greater enthusiasm in overcoming the difficulties; and, from some of the combinations so formed, new social groupings of scholars might arise, giving a permanent redefinition of boundaries and a new shape to the map of knowledge.

A NOTE ON TEACHING METHODS

The extent and quality of research on teaching methods in higher education leave much to be desired, and many methods persist because they are traditional to an institution, or because they reproduce what the teacher himself received, rather than because they have been closely studied and proved effective. However, it is not at all easy to monitor the efficiency of teaching methods, for the final, and imperfect, measurement by examination success relates to a state of education which is the consequence of the private work of the student as well as of the package of formal teaching which he has received.

I have referred elsewhere to the inefficiency necessarily arising from the application of standardized teaching packages to heterogeneous students (p. 31). In addition, there are some points which need to be made about the contents of the teaching package.

Teaching methods of course depend on the subject. It may help to begin with a subject, such as history, in which a student might in principle attain a reasonable standard simply by intelligent and assiduous reading in libraries. (Some students have certainly done this, and not only in 'external' courses.) But most students are not capable of organizing their studies to achieve success in this way, and most students lack the motivation to work in isolation. The *lecture* (that is, an oration by a teacher with no opportunity for students to enter into discussion) may appear to be simply a spoken textbook, and sometimes this is a literal description of it – the lecturer reads from a text which he uses unchanged from year to year, and which he may publish. However, it performs three functions. First, the personal presence of the lecturer, his idiosyncrasies and jokes, even his failings, create an interest and a motivation which the written word does not generally provide; or, at least, the variation of communication, some in words and some in writing, gives a more effective package than the use of one channel only. Second, the lecturer can help the student to organize his studies: these, he will say, are the key issues of this subject, and here is a list of the further reading which should enable you to gain a fuller understanding. Third, the lecturer can convey knowledge or attitudes too recently developed to be obtainable from text books.

Lectures appear to be an effective means of achieving these results up to a considerable size of audience. So long as the lecturer can be heard, and can be seen well enough to convey his personality, he can be simultaneously 'received' by a large number of students. For this reason, some commentators have supposed that higher education is an industry with large economies of scale: double your numbers, double the size of all the lecture classes, and you need few if any more staff. The objection to this, of course, is that other kinds of teaching, without this scope for economy, are also needed. Anyway, in practical terms, lectures usually have to be used very 'inefficiently' (that is to say, with a much smaller audience than would be capable of receiving the message) because the student body splits into so many diverse interest groups. Some of the remaining large audiences ought, in fact, to be divided, because they are achieved by bringing together students with a different background of preparation or with different personality characteristics; they offend against the principle that each act of teaching should be planned to fit its students.

The remainder of formal teaching in history will be in small groups, variously called seminars or tutorials or supervisions or discussion groups. These groups extend the influence of the teacher in organising the work of the student, for instance by requiring specific pieces of written work to be prepared. They provide the student with an indication of his progress, as written work is discussed and marked. Most importantly, they stimulate the student's thinking by question and answer and by the expectation that he will contribute to discussion; and they give each student an opportunity of clearing up difficulties which he has found in his studies.

Some of this interchange can be 'automated' (see p. 127), though perhaps not, with any economy or advantage, in history. In many areas small-group teaching by a human teacher appears to be absolutely essential to the educational process as we understand it in Britain; the question is how much there should be. It is probable that *more* small-group teaching, and in smaller groups (provided there are enough people present to produce a good discussion) will produce an improvement of performance over the whole range which is in any way conceivable as a practical possibility – up, say, to the point of twice-weekly meetings in groups of two for each course, which would be far beyond the capacity of most higher education institutions. There is evidence that teaching in *large* discussion groups is patchy in its effects, because some students, and probably those most in need of help, will sit on the back row and opt out of the discussion. What we do not know is the balance between improvement in performance and cost: weekly meetings are better than fortnightly meetings, but are they sufficiently better to justify the doubling of the input of staff time to this activity? And, returning to a point made above, it must always be remembered that our judgement of an improvement in education is usually quantifiable only by using the proxy of success in examinations, which (as will be seen in the next chapter) are imperfect measures of ill-defined qualities.

The forms of teaching used in science involve, of course, practical work in the laboratory or in the field. This is partly an occasion for gaining familiarity with experimental methods, and for 'learning by doing' – just as the mathematician learns by solving problems, and the historian by writing an essay which requires him to construct judgements not capable of immediate copying from the textbook. Practical classes are also, however, an occasion for discussion between teacher and student, and perform part of the functions of a tutorial class in history. This is why it is unfortunate if their supervision is skimped or delegated to people who have little direct concern with other teaching.

Another aspect of teaching method is the stimulation given to the student by set work – essays, problems, practical work, projects. Here ignorance pursues us further. A good piece of set work is plainly one which forces the student into unaccustomed paths of thought – that is, which cannot be answered in a standard manner by looking up a textbook. For some types of set work, such as writing essays on a historical subject, the student will learn more the longer the time he gives, within reason; for others, such as solving mathematical problems, this is not generally so. The decision about an optimum workload involves a choice between stimulating the student at many points, but leaving him insufficient time to deal with any subject in depth, and giving him a few tasks, with a danger that, over important areas of the subject, he will remain unstimulated. Ingenuity in the invention of set work questions can help to reconcile these alternatives, but it can be costly in the time of the teachers. Furthermore, the choice just outlined is made within another one, about the division of the student's time between formal teaching (lectures, tutorials, practical work), doing set work, and studying on his own initiative. This choice evidently requires a judgement about the capacity of students to work: is it right to press them hard or 'stretch' them (with a danger that some will collapse), or should a more modest limit be set? On all these choices we have little hard evidence.

It follows that I am not able to make specific proposals about the balance of teaching methods in the year 2000; it is necessary instead to propose that, during the next twenty years, there should be much more serious research on the whole matter. This would make it possible to propose, with conviction, that those who teach in higher education should, like school-teachers, be required to learn their trade. The weakness so far of attempts to make training in higher education teaching a general policy has been the difficulty of giving any convincing answer as to what the training should include.

7

WHY AND HOW TO EXAMINE

When I was a student at Cambridge, I took in my second year the examination for the course called the Second Part of the Mathematical Tripos, attaining the status which, since the eighteenth century, has been called a Wrangler – that is, what is elsewhere described as first class honours. The students of the year were divided into Wranglers, Senior Optimes, Junior Optimes, those considered to deserve various credits for an ordinary degree, and failures, by an examination whose papers consisted of sections of 'bookwork' or theory to be reproduced, each followed by a problem of considerable difficulty. Candidates were invited to do as many questions as they could, with the reminder that complete answers to questions scored more than fragments. Such a system produces an enormous range of results, from the weak candidates who can memorise some pieces of bookwork but lack the facility to apply it, and thus get credit only for a few fragments, to the genius who completes the entire paper, with solutions better than his examiners had devised. My experience suggests that answers to about half the paper were adequate for the top class. Most of the candidates must have failed to solve most of the problems – a fact easily and unequivocally recognizable; some will have got an answer, but by a clumsy method, in which case rather more judgement would be required from the examiner.

When, after a further year's (or rather, eight months') study. I took an abbreviated version of the second part of the Economics Tripos, I faced an examination of quite a different kind. The number of questions to be attempted was prescribed; the answers were to be essays intended to show a general command of the subject. It would be possible, of course, to give a wrong answer, but even weak students could manage to disguise their ignorance by ingenious waffling: on the other hand, even a strong student could hardly produce a polished reply in half an hour, and I doubt if the examiners were often required to recognize an answer better than they would have given themselves. Such a system produces a narrow range of results – though this can be to some extent disguised where, as at Cambridge at that time, a non-numerical system of marking is used. Furthermore, the mark given (provided the answer is not wholly perverse or wrong) depends on points of style and method which will be assessed differently by different examiners. In fact, experiments show that different examiners, or the same examiner at widely separated times, can give very different marks to the same essay. This produces an uncertainty which is to some extent 'averaged out' over the whole examination, or reduced by double marking, but which nevertheless casts doubt on the fairness of the system.

Fortunately Cambridge, having specialized degrees, does not normally attempt to combine marks for mathematical problems with those for essays. In other institutions of higher education, however, it is by no means unknown for such combinations of unstandardized marks (that is, marks varying over very different ranges) to be made – with results excessively unfavourable to weak candidates for the 'mathematics' type of paper, which would include various science subjects, and excessively favourable to those who can bring in a ninety per cent from such a paper, when fellow-students doing essay questions only rarely exceed seventy per cent. Even at Cambridge, I must admit with regret that (according to my supervisor) my placing in the Economics Tripos was due to the advantage of a high mark in an optional paper in mathematical statistics: which suggests that my entire career would have been different if I had chosen a different option.

Factors such as these do not enhance trust in the systems of examination common in higher education; and indeed these systems are commonly much less sophisticated in method, and much less carefully monitored, than those used by the Examining Boards in the schools. They are, of course, largely free from favouritism or jobbery, because most institutions give the final power to determine marginal cases to an external examiner, who is usually a senior member of staff of another university or college. This has the great advantage of producing, across the United Kingdom, an approximate equality of standards, at a particular time, for comparable qualifications. No words from an external examiner are more persuasive than 'That chap would have got a Third in my department.' The presence of the external examiner also protects candidates from the idiosyncrasies of their chief teachers. In school examinations the guidelines set by an examiner are sometimes allowed to have, on a matter of taste or preference, a binding force which they do not deserve.

However, the equality of standards thus achieved is only approximate; it depends on fallible memories in attempting to achieve consistency from year to year; and it cannot pretend to provide consistency between subjects. Science degree subjects very commonly yield a larger harvest of results at the first class honours level than the humanities, despite the fact that, in recent years, the average standard at entry has been lower for science. This difference is unlikely to be due to superior teaching; it might be ascribed to a difference of standard, though it is not easy to give a precise meaning to such a concept, but most probably it is the unacknowledged result of the difference in the spread of marks between subjects where answers are right or wrong and those where they convey one of many possible opinions.

But even if one could deal with faults of method and uncertainties of assessment, a more serious problem remains. What is being examined? To whom are the results addressed, and what information do they properly convey? In a long experience, I have rarely found satisfactory answers to these questions; and this raises a doubt about the justification for having examinations at all.

Until recently, the final examination for a degree, diploma or certificate was commonly brief but arduous: six hours of frantic scribbling on several consecutive days, interspersed in some subjects by long practicals. Such an examination establishes the presence or absence of stamina, of the ability to put forth great effort on varied subjects in a short time. It also tests some matters of lesser importance, such as the ability to write very rapidly without becoming completely illegible, and the ability to do arithmetic or algebra quickly without making silly mistakes. But as a means of making judgements *between* candidates it is manifestly unfair. It ignores the possibility that biological rhythms will affect candidates in different ways; and it exalts speed and stamina, and the possession of a retentive memory, at least for the days or hours since the final revision, over good judgement and wise appreciation of the subject.

Many institutions have therefore diluted the concentrated final examination by bringing in marks based on 'continuous assessment', that is, in practice, on a series of tasks undertaken during the last year or two of the course. Such tasks can be free of the narrow time-limits of an examination, and can test (for instance) ability to use a wide range of literature. It was originally argued that such a method of assessment would cause much less stress, being spread over a long period, and would thus be a fairer indication of the 'normal' performance of the student rather than what he could do in a special and arduous situation. In fact, the evidence suggests that being examined every few weeks often produces more stress than the concentrated final examination, so the argument does not succeed. It is indeed possible to use continuous assessment to provide a more subtle appreciation of qualities than can be obtained from the old final examination, but only at the cost of serious disadvantages. The system is unfair to candidates whose work has been improving, because it brings in lower marks from an earlier time, and unduly generous to candidates whose work has a declining trend. This is because the result of a 'final' examination will be assumed to relate to a final state – that is, it measures 'quality of output' – and no one would expect it to refer to an average state over some unspecified period. The tasks set will seldom be as well-defined, or as carefully examined, as the questions in a final examination. Many of them are likely to be of such a nature that there is no assurance that the work submitted is the candidate's unaided effort; so that what is examined may be the corporate wisdom of a number of groups of friends and collaborators, or even something drawn from a file of answers known to have found favour in earlier years.

It will help to decide what ought to be done if we first enquire what would be lost if examinations were abolished. To this there are three answers:

1   *If there were no intermediate examinations (or at least, systematic schemes for marking work) during the course, the student would have no way of assessing his progress, and might accept standards of work which are very much lower than the course intends.*

2   *Examinations provide, for some candidates and perhaps for many, an important element of motivation. This judgement lies behind the growth of 'classifying', which has led to most degrees becoming classified honours degrees, while many sub-degree qualifications, even if nominally on a pass-fail basis, have developed classes of 'merit' and 'distinction'. The motivational power of a pure pass-fail qualification is limited, since most candidates can readily pass, and get nothing more however well they perform.*

3   *Examinations provide evidence of the student's quality which is of value to his future employers, and to himself, in making a choice of career.*

These are all quite sensible answers, but they do not point the same way. The first points to the need for a system of diagnostic testing, which can help students to judge their progress and also help with intermediate choices of course, such as often have to be made after the first year. The second implies that the candidate enters a friendly contest or match with his fellow-students; the rules of the game must be clear, and the result a fair one under the rules. To provide something to strive for, the result must also be unequivocal. The third answer implies that the student and his potential employers should receive such information about his qualities as can properly and justly be deduced from his performance. There is no sense at all in losing some of this information by combining it all into a single class-mark.

In the light of all this, what advice can we give to potential examiners in the year 2000? The first element is, I suggest, 'Never examine without a clear purpose, and a clear idea of how you are achieving that purpose.' It must be possible, not only to define the qualities which it is desired to test, but also to show how the examination in fact tests those qualities. It is no use pretending that you are testing ability to marshal an independent argument if in practice you reserve the highest marks for those who regurgitate accurately what their lecturers have said. The question should have been framed in a way not capable of being answered directly from the book or the lecture notes. Although it is often impracticable, there is something to be said for having a rule that an examination should be set and marked, internally, by people who have had no hand in teaching the course concerned; for the temptation to give too much credit for the possession of a good memory is a frequent one.

The only good purpose of examining or testing *during* a course is to advise, admonish, and, in the extreme case, eject the student. Such examinations or tests should be few; they should be scientifically designed to yield the necessary diagnostic information – Has this man or woman mastered the mathematical methods which will be essential to the understanding of next year's course in physics?: the results should generally be confidential between the student and his teachers, though the methods used must be publicly known, so that they can be accepted as fair. Generally, the examinations should be so phased that those who are found wanting can go back and catch up. In fact, they may be best subdivided into numerous sectional tests, so that diagnostic examining becomes part of a programmed learning approach.

I believe that there is a value in using the competitive spirit as an aid to motivation, but that a single contest at the end of the course is enough – it is overdoing it to have competitive examinations at frequent intervals. That contest should be put in its place; it should not be the sole public result of taking the course, but should be seen as mainly a ranking relative to fellow-students, like a place in a class in those schools which still have such placings. (The argument that it is harmful to tell a weak student that he is bottom of the class does not, I think, have much validity in higher education, which is not a compulsory activity). There is no harm in setting the ranking against a grid which purports to show absolute standards, consistent from year to year, provided that it is made clear that what is really being shown is a standard which is more or less consistent over a short period of years. 'We rank you in the Third Class, and we think you would have been in the same class last year or the year before, so the ranking is not an accidental result of having some clever competitors this year.'

A contest of this kind, however, must be scrupulously fair. It must contain no element in which unauthorized group work, or plagiarism, can easily enter. The result must not depend on accidents of subject choice, as when unstandardized marks with differing ranges are combined. So far as possible, the contest must be seen to test qualities which the student knows to be important, rather than mere memory or speed in writing. It must be as fair as possible to those who have been ill or disturbed, but must test all candidates at the same point or points in the course.

All this points to a modified form of the concentrated final examination. The modifications might be:

1 To split the examination into two parts six weeks apart, so that the results are not so much influenced by the candidates' state of health during a single week.

2 To diversify the methods of examination, as is already

done in some places, for example, by using multiple choice questions, or allowing specified reference books to be used, or allowing a substantial time for a detailed answer to a question, so that the results are less dependent on good memory, quick recall and rapid writing.

3 To standardize the marks for each subject, that is, bring them to a common standard deviation or 'spread', before combining them into an overall rating.

The examination should however remain formal and supervised, the questions being secret until the time of answering, since otherwise there is insufficient assurance of fairness between candidates.

The class or rank obtained from such an examination might be entered on the final certificate given to the student and available for his use in seeking employment, but, since the university or college will have much more relevant information than is contained in a single class-mark, it should give some of that information too. Some qualities of the student, or special factors which have affected his performance, will be best described in a personal reference; but the certificate should carry the things which can be expressed in a standard form, such as marks or classes in the different subjects or course studied. In fact, the student should be provided with a *profile* from which can be seen the range of his studies, the strong subjects and the weak ones, whether he has been gaining strength in his studies or losing it. It would of course not be easy to make this profile intelligible to its potential users, but the task is not impossible; there is no reason why substantial explanations should not be appended.

One result of making the 'public certificate' into a profile would be to force examiners to consider what it is that the outside world needs to know, rather than what is traditional in a subject or can most easily be examined. Thus an accountant or a doctor needs a certificate of achievement of knowledge; the world requires an assurance that he or she has studied certain subjects and has, to a sufficient degree, mastered them. But the profile should also give evidence of aptitude, that is, of potential for future development, such as may be shown by ingenuity in devising a course of action in an unfamiliar situation; this is the analogy of testing a mathematician by problems as well as his memory of bookwork. In music technical knowledge, aesthetic judgement and ability in performance are all relevant qualities, for which separate assessments should be made; and so for other subjects. It would be a considerable advance if, by the year 2000, we had removed the single final class-mark or certificate of passing from its undue prominence, and, in the process of substituting a detailed profile, had forced examiners to think clearly about the qualities being tested, and the relevance of testing them.

Some, however, would see an even greater advance in abolishing examinations altogether, at least in subjects where it is thought that employers do not really need the information; or in confining the scope of competitive testing to those students who ask to be allowed to enter the competition. But there are some serious difficulties in this selective approach. If one looks at the flow from higher education into employment, it is very difficult to identify any subject-area for which no certification of standards is needed. Teachers of arts subjects sometimes think that the scientists need this certification, while their students do not; but they forget the importance of certification for aspiring teachers, civil servants and many others. In the absence of degree classes, how would the award of support to take a higher degree be handled? It is naïve to suppose that this support could be made available to anyone on demand, or could depend entirely on that notoriously fallible instrument, the letter of personal recommendation. Furthermore, the existence of tests of performance provides some assurance to the taxpayer that the considerable support for higher education is not being wastefully used; that students who are idle are identified, and suffer the disadvantage of being seen to have failed. Indeed, a system without examinations could only be tolerable if entry to higher education was freely available to anyone. There would certainly be a public outcry if idle students were seen to be occupying places and suffering no disadvantage, while others more assiduous waited unsatisfied at the gate. For these reasons, it seems to me more practical to concentrate on the reform of examining, rather than its total or selective abolition.

8

RESEARCH AND PUBLIC SERVICE

Owing to the use of words which are not clearly defined, a considerable mythology has grown up about the relation of research to higher education. University teachers tend to believe that research and teaching are inseparable, like mutton and wool on a sheep; the historically minded will explain that this great principle was imported from Wilhelm von Humboldt's reform of the Prussian universities in the nineteenth century, with the implication that in earlier years the English and Scottish universities neglected research. Teachers in other parts of higher education usually pay lip service at least to the necessity of research, occasionally developing it to become a substantial user of their time. Those who have no research record tend to be somewhat ashamed of the fact, and will explain that they hope to get started on something shortly.

In ordinary speech, 'research' is a process of discovering new knowledge. It gives us, after a further process of 'development', new drugs, or faster travel, or new sources of energy. With perhaps a little difficulty, people could be persuaded to include non-scientific examples, such as the discovery of a forgotten Shakespeare play, or the development of a new system in philosophy, or the derivation of rules of behaviour in accounting for multi-national companies. However, the usage in higher education is vaguer than this. Since it is considered to be right for university teachers to do 'research', and to regard it as a claimant on their time of equal importance with teaching, the word has tended to become a portmanteau one, carrying most of the things which teachers and their

93

institutions do in the course of employment but outside teaching time. It will be better to release the various meanings carried in this portmanteau to appear under their own titles.

1 *Scholarship* is the possession of an extensive and profound knowledge of a subject, to be obtained by studying its literature or by discussion with other scholars. Thus the 'research' time of a teacher of classics is likely to be spent in reading widely in classical literature and in commentaries and critical works about it.

2 *Theory construction* is the activity of developing a logical structure by applying operations to defined entities, the system being constrained by prior assumptions. This is the work of the pure mathematician, and similar activities in other subjects can very often be set out in mathematical form; for instance, the construction of economic 'models', and indeed the whole of economic theory, can be regarded as a (rather pedestrian) subsection of mathematics, gaining interest only when tested as an explanation of the real world.

3 *Observing and chronicling* is the recording of natural phenomena, human reactions, historical events and the like, in a manner which so far as possible preserves the record uninfluenced by the presence of the observer. We can include here also the detective operation, familiar to historians, of deducing from imperfect and partial primary records a more comprehensive and satisfactory secondary record.

4 *Experiment* is the recording of phenomena in a situation which has been created and planned by the observer. This is a typical activity of some, though not of course of all, of the sciences; the chemist experiments, but the astronomer observes. A particular form of experiment is the *repetitive test*, in which a large number of possibilities are 'screened' in order to identify one or more with desired properties; this is, for instance, a common method of research into pharmaceuticals.

5 *Theory testing* is the confrontation of theoretical hypotheses with the results of observation or of experiment, in order to decide whether a theory provides an adequate explanation, and can thus be selected as a basis for further development or for prediction.

6   *Design* is the use of known principles to derive a specification for a new creation. Thus the research of an architect might take the form of designing an energy-saving house; or an engineer might design an installation for extracting power from the waves of the sea.

7   *Development* is the process of taking a result established in small-scale experiment, or embodied in a preliminary design, through the stages which lead to an actual application. It is not of course normally an activity of higher education, but some 'research' in higher education is concerned with assisting industrial or other users to overcome particular problems in the development process.

8   *Criticising and elucidating* is a common activity in the literary subjects, and an occasional one elsewhere. It is a hybrid, in part an extension of scholarship and observation, and in part an exercise in artistic judgement.

9   *Artistic creation* is not properly 'research', but is likely to be substituted for it as a use of the time of some of those who teach art, music and drama, and of some 'creative writers' in the literary subjects.

10   *Consulting and advising*, a typical activity of business studies departments, though it is also found in other subjects, may involve new theory, observation, experiment and testing, but may simply be an application of methods and principles already known to a particular need.

Dangers of misunderstanding and of misuse of resources arise from lumping all these uses of time together as 'research'. Thus, it is not true that teachers in higher education are necessarily concerned with exploring 'new frontiers of knowledge'. This is an illegitimate extension to all subjects of a typical activity of the scientific experimenter or observer. Much 'research' is the discovery *by the researcher* of something which already existed and was part of the body of scholarship; perhaps followed by a reinterpretation of the discovery for the benefit of others in the present generation. The 'frontiers of knowledge' concept has led to an unhelpful emphasis on original discovery, so that a young lecturer in French thinks it proper 'research' to do a critical edition of a justly forgotten minor poet, but not to spend his time obtaining a profounder understanding of the great figures of French literature. (The degree of Ph.D. can be obtained by 'original research' of an unimportant kind, but not by depth of scholarship alone.) Furthermore, it has not been helpful to disguise the application of knowledge, which may be much the best use of the time of some scholars, as its discovery.

There is no reason or evidence to support a belief that all the things which people do with 'research' time will benefit their teaching, or will receive benefit from it. However, the argument, as it is usually presented, depends heavily on the example of the natural sciences: liveliness in teaching, it is said, is encouraged by the activity of observing, experimenting and testing theory on the frontiers of knowledge; and therefore research in this sense should be a major part of the activity of all higher education institutions. I know of no proof of this argument, and from my own observations I take liberty to doubt it. Of course people of great ability, if placed in a situation where both teaching and research are expected, will often do both of them well. But the correlation which seems to me more significant is between 'scholarship' and good teaching. The truly learned man, drawing from knowledge much more extensive and profound than that expected of his students, has a quality which is recognized and which has a strong educational influence, even if expressed in halting words. Because of the extent of his knowledge, the learned man or 'scholar' normally has a good judgement of what is important and can set things in their right proportion. No doubt he will at some points have reached the 'frontiers of knowledge', in the sense of knowing the latest and most advanced work, but it is not essential that he should himself be pushing those frontiers further out. Indeed, very few teachers are making contributions to knowledge which are of enough significance to matter in their teaching. It is sometimes argued that the act of discovery is a means of keeping the teacher awake, and that otherwise he will go on teaching from out-of-date material.

But the active scholar always has more work to do, journals to be followed, new developments to be mastered. This is the essential activity for keeping teaching fresh.

In this perspective, what happened in the nineteenth century was the assimilation into the universities of a new set of scientific activities, previously carried on by private gentlemen who dabbled in natural philosophy. It is not surprising that, in the infancy of a science, the excitement of new discovery claims the main attention. The teacher could know all that there was to be known about his subject, and still have time to use in expanding its narrow circumference. The student, too, could rapidly assimilate much of what was already known, and join in the pleasures of discovery. But it was an illegitimate assumption that this close partnership of teaching and scientific investigation was essential or desirable in all subjects and at all times. Indeed, in the sciences themselves, the enormous expansion of knowledge means that discoverers are working on a tiny section of a long circumference, and what they do may be remote from their teaching interests except in relation to a few research students. The discoverer is in danger of becoming a man who 'knows more and more about less and less', and for inspiration in teaching it is better to turn to the scientific scholar, that is, the man whose knowledge of the science is broad as well as profound, so that he sees the interrelations of its parts.

The substitution of 'scholarship' for the imprecise word 'research' as the necessary adjunct of teaching would have substantial consequences for the future of higher education. In universities and colleges of every kind, time would be allowed and resources allocated to encourage members of the teaching staff to become genuinely learned men. What other activities were undertaken – of theorising, observing, experimenting, designing, developing, consulting, creating – could be decided according to the need for each activity and the suitability of the institution to perform it. There would be no presumption that, if the number of students of physics doubles, research (that is, theorising, experimenting, and theory-testing) in physics in the higher education institutions should also double: that is the wrong way to determine the amount and placing of such research.

There are in fact some sorts of experimental activity which, because of the concentration of resources which they require, are best centred in national or international laboratories or research stations. Other types of 'research' or development require a closeness to the potential user which is not likely to be achieved by scattering them across higher education institutions. This is a category which should not be regarded as confined to science and technology in some of their more specialized industrial applications: certain types of research on future government policies, for instance, are best conducted in a close relation to those who understand the political and administrative problems of applying a new policy.

There is a cynical view that all the activities which come within the broad definition of 'research' are a perquisite of the university teacher, which teachers in other colleges would also like to acquire: that they are, in fact a grant of the freedom to do very much what one likes for half the year, and without this freedom there would be difficulty in attracting enough talent to the academic profession. I see no evidence to support this cynicism. On the contrary: although of course a lot of academics value the freedom, there are others, and they may even be in a majority, who pursue research and allied activities without great conviction, because it is expected of them and it is believed that promotion depends mainly on the research record – especially those parts of it which are published. Such people would be happier if they could, with a good conscience, spend more time on deepening their scholarship without having to lengthen a list of publications; or even spend more time on teaching. There is an implication, of course, that promotion should no longer depend on the publication record – for some excellent scholars publish very little. This might have the beneficial results of relieving the world of a mass of unnecessary publication, and of relieving teachers of a cause of worry and discontent.

In the year 2000, then, there might be a much more unequal distribution of true research facilities, some subjects relying mainly on research centres outside higher education, and the work within universities and colleges being, where appropriate, concentrated in a few places. This new distribution could most readily be achieved by separating the research budget from the teaching budget, and making decisions about the placing of research money on their own merits, largely uninfluenced by the distribution of teaching resources, which may depend on a short-lived fashion of student preference.

In other words, research in general would be treated as expensive forms of science (nuclear physics, radioastronomy and the like) are already treated. There are problems of undue centralization of power in this, but they can, I believe, be overcome. A more unequal distribution of facilities would benefit graduate teaching, which at present is in some scientific and technological subjects spread over far too many centres. The research grants to teaching institutions would pay for equipment, materials, full time research workers, and ancillary staff, and possibly for the extra costs arising from the release of members of the teaching staff from some of their normal teaching load. In addition, all institutions would have funds to make ample provision for the pursuit of scholarship, and in particular for travel to the great libraries and the main centres of research.

I must make it clear that I am *not* arguing for a major reduction of the central research activities of theorising, observing and experimenting within higher education, but for a firm decision to concentrate them – which implies that there would be no provision for their funding in other places. Furthermore, I am not arguing that a particular institution (say, the University of Cambridge) should be recognized *in toto* as a centre to receive funds for whatever kind of research it chooses to do. Such a system would be inconsistent with concentration: it could be (to take a ridiculous example) that Cambridge is not appropriately chosen as among the best dozen centres for economic research, and it should have no right to claim public funds for its development. However, the concentration would mainly affect funds for what might be called 'research institutes' – the centres of co-operative research which employ full-time research staff, and which may use their own buildings, equipment and ancillary staff. Much of what is *called* 'research' is really the pursuit of scholarship by individual teachers, and provision for this (with its ancillary expenses) would not only continue, but should properly be more generous than at present.

One consequence of a clearer policy on research might be to set free activities such as design, development and consultancy from their present status as users of research time, which sometimes results in giving them an unhelpful disguise as 'original discovery', and to encourage universities and colleges to develop them on their own merits wherever this seems to be an appropriate use of resources. Indeed, the claimant on resources, after the needs of teaching and scholarship are met, should not be a portmanteau concept of 'research', but rather the public service which institutions which employ considerable brain-power should be expected to give. This is a point more clearly understood in the U.S. than it is here. The service can be of a very varied kind, and the following are offered only as examples of work which could be a natural growth from the work of a higher education institution:

1   *Development and testing of the results of research, and even the subsequent manufacture and sale of the developed product, if continued oversight by the researchers is important.*

2   *Sale on licence of knowledge about developed products and processes.*

3   *Testing services which use knowledge special to the institution or enable equipment already provided to be more fully used.*

4   *Use by outsiders of spare time on other equipment, for example electron microscopes or computers.*

5   *Provision of consultancy services in scientific, technological or business subjects to industry, commerce and public or charitable bodies.*

6   *Advice services to institutions with comparable functions, for example, on teaching methods, assessment, library organization.*

7   *Use by the public of library and similar resources, including films, tapes, bibliographical advice.*

8   *Provision of specialist assistance with regional or local planning.*

9   *Work on local and regional history, and the guardianship of archives or of archaeological sites.*

10 *Service to school teaching by making known the results of research and assisting with experiment.*

11 *Provision of laboratory-based language teaching services.*

12 *Acting as a centre for the arts – music, fine art, theatre; including the provision of public galleries and museums, and of concerts, plays, film showings, record libraries, etc., etc.; providing a base for touring theatre companies and groups of musicians.*

13 *Using land, buildings or resources for demonstration projects in the social services or for the general improvement of social conditions in the neighbourhood.*

The principle which should, I believe, be asserted in relation to such forms of service is that the institution should actively seek to develop them wherever they are appropriate, and should equip itself with appropriate administrative organs for doing so. This is an attitude to be distinguished from that which allows public service to arise as an accidental consequence of the interests of a few individuals. There are many good things in universities and colleges which deserve to be more widely shared, but this will not happen unless there is a positive policy to seek out and encourage the sharing. Of course, what can be done will be limited, both by the lack of money which can properly be used for purposes other than teaching and scholarship, and by the existence at a particular place of other bodies and institutions which can perform some of the services better or more appropriately. But in my view what can be done exceeds by a large margin what has so far been accepted as a satisfactory standard of public service.

9

THE GOVERNMENT AND FINANCE OF HIGHER EDUCATION

By far the greater part of higher education is paid for by the state. There are reasons, which are explored later in this chapter, why it may be better not to have a totally free service; but there is no realistic possibility of 'returning higher education to private enterprise', for this would be so large a change that it could not be achieved without serious social injustice and economic disruption. I therefore assume that the state will continue to be the main paymaster.

By what we like to suppose to be a typically British expedient, the paymaster has kept in the background, exercising a general control over budgets and a more specific one over capital programmes, but leaving a great deal of discretion in day-to-day operation to the individual institutions. For the universities, an intermediary body (the University Grants Committee), largely drawn from the universities themselves, divides up the total grant between the recipients and offers general advice. Within the budget available to them, however, the individual universities act much as if they were competitive private enterprise units, and in particular their Senates assume a high degree of freedom in deciding what to teach and what students to admit. For most of the public sector colleges, the financial responsibility is exercised by local authorities, even if most of the money is eventually found from central funds. This, as noted in Chapter 1, tends to lead to a closer control of some details, such as the number of secretarial staff, in order to avoid inconsistencies within the local authority service; but, although the essential academic decisions may need the concurrence of outside bodies such as the Regional Advisory Council and the CNAA, they are in general initiated within the college, and strong principals manage to obtain a wide freedom of action for their institutions.

Throughout higher education the normal pattern in major institutions is to have a two-headed system of government: a Council or Board of Governors or their equivalent having final legal responsibility for assets and employment, and dealing with finance and buildings; and a Senate or Academic Board or their equivalent making or initiating the academic decisions. The academic staff is represented on the Council or Board of Governors, and so, in most places, are the students; but it is rare for the 'lay' (that is, non-academic) interests to have any voice on the Senate or Academic Board. The predominant pattern is to have a 'lay' majority on the Council, but the ancient universities of Oxford and Cambridge are in practice controlled by their academic staff for most purposes: they are workers' co-operatives.

There are historical reasons for two-headed government, and it is often seen by academics as enabling them to decide the matters which interest them without interference. But that freedom can be stated more unkindly as a freedom to make academic decisions without taking any notice of the views of the wider community which pays the bills, employs the graduates and uses the research. In fact, 'lay' members would probably have a much more useful contribution to make to the design of courses than to the design of buildings, and I find it impossible to think of a reputable reason why this contribution should be prevented. Furthermore, there is no proper line of division between an academic decision and one which relates to finance, or to buildings, or personnel. They are related parts of a single whole, and the body which presumes to govern an institution should see and, so far as possible, have under control the full implications of each decision.

These are powerful arguments, and I have not seen them receive a satisfactory direct answer. Some of the sentiment in favour of a two-headed system is related to the conservative principle that it is safer: foolish measures which go unchecked in the Senate or Academic Board can be defeated, perhaps on financial grounds, in the Council or Board of Governors. There is substance in this point, for higher education institutions are sometimes tempted to take very foolish decisions, perhaps under the influence of a passing fashion or in deference to some powerful extreme group. But there are alternative ways of providing for a delaying or revising function, and it should be noted that a less desirable effect of the two-headed system is to increase greatly the power of the chief executive of the institution. Any intelligent Vice-Chancellor or Principal soon learns how to use divided control in order to get his own way, arranging that when something which he dislikes passes in one body it will be questioned in the other.

Another line of argument in favour of the *status quo* is that the agenda of the academic body is too long and detailed to be understood by lay members. This is often true, but what it means is that the supreme academic body, which ought to give itself time to 'see the wood for the trees' and to debate issues of principle, is allowing itself to be submerged by a mass of detail which ought to be done by sub-committees. Nor is it convincing to point to the considerable discontent which has followed a notable experiment in unitary government, that at the University of Toronto, for this experiment appears to have been fatally flawed by the development of a bureaucratic system which greatly slowed down business. I believe that in practice the widespread support for the two-headed system derives almost entirely, not from rational argument, but from the belief of academics that they know best, even on issues where, on a wider view, it is very evident that they could benefit by listening to the voice of those with a different experience.

I recommend, therefore, a development – between now and the year 2000 – of 'unitary' government, by a single governing Council for each institution assisted by a number of sub-committees for specific purposes. In that Council the number of members external and internal to the institution should be equal, so that neither group could safely act without considering the views of the other. This would provide the internal members with an ultimate safeguard against being overridden on a point of principle on which they are agreed, but without sacrificing the advantage of getting the views of external people on academic matters. On the ordinary run of business, however, the danger of deadlock due to the balanced composition of the governing Council would not be great, because there would be a variety of participants in both the internal and the external group, and a regular 'voting pattern' is not likely. We must next consider who these participants should be.

The question 'who should participate in the government of a higher education institution?' can be answered in two quite different ways, one concerned with the *interests* of the participants and the other with their *contribution*. A long list of people can claim an interest in the results of the work done or in the way in which it is run, including:

1 *The national government, or representative taxpayers, who provide most of the money*
2 *The local authorities, or representative ratepayers, who also contribute, or administer state-derived funds, or have a responsibility in management*
3 *Private founders and benefactors*
4 *The employers of graduates or other students completing courses*
5 *The users of applied research (if this is a function of the institution)*
6 *The users of other services from the institution, for example, consultancy and testing*
7 *The 'learned community' – for example, the Royal Society and the British Academy, with an interest in the effectiveness of pure research, if this is a significant part of the work of the institution*
8 *The schools, with an interest in opportunities for their pupils and in their fair treatment*
9 *Parents of students*

10 *Present students, as 'consumers' of the services*
11 *Past students, as persons with an interest in the good name and success of their* alma mater
12 *Employees of every grade, who have an interest in good employment practices as well as in the general good name of the institution*
13 *Representatives of linked institutions – for instance, those receiving students for further training, sharing a joint system of validation of qualifications, or undertaking joint courses*
14 *External examiners*
15 *Representatives of those who have an interest in higher education apart from its value in employment – for example, societies with a cultural interest*
16 *Representatives of the surrounding community, on which the institution has an economic and social impact*
17 *General community representatives, in their capacity not as taxpayers but as persons with a broad interest in educational or research or cultural policy*
18 *People interested in equal opportunity for the sexes and for students and employees of all racial origins*

Even allowing for the possibility that one member could represent several interests (for example, by appointing a black female local government councillor with an interest in medical research and children of higher education student age) it is difficult to see how a satisfactory governing body could be created from so many interests. Some would require several representatives (for instance, to achieve adequate coverage of grades and interests among employees, especially as the Union and non-Union group might require separate representation). Considerations of balance would then require several representatives under other heads, and the total would rise to a hundred or more. With a very large governing body, the initiating power tends to pass to unacknowledged groups of officers meeting in private. This produces a divergence between the formal and the informal structure of government, which eventually may lead to misunderstanding, suspicion and conflct.

However, the list of those with evident competence to make a significant contribution to the decisions to be made can be set down more briefly:

1   *Educationalists, including experienced teachers and administrators from the institution itself, from other similar places, and from the school system*

2   *Educated men and women, and especially those who are brought into contact with higher education because of their interest in general cultural matters, or as employers of graduates, or as users of research or other services*

3   *Managers who can advise on the management of the institution's affairs*

4   *To a limited extent, students, since (despite their lack of experience) they may have relevant things to say about the needs and aspirations of their successors*

Any structure of government will evidently be a compromise, but, given the danger of producing an unworkably large Council, it seems best to give the principle of competence priority over that of representativeness. Even so, there are problems of finding appropriate 'constituencies' to appoint those who serve. Members of local authorities, for instance, are 'representative citizens' only in a special sense: they are representative members of the group of those citizens who are prepared to engage in political activity at a local level. Similarly, students appointed to governing bodies may not be representative of the majority of students, who opt out of the political process; there has sometimes been a heavy over-representation of extreme left-wing groups. Any scheme of government must, if it is to be plausible, do its best to solve this problem of 'constituencies'.

Chapter 5 recommended a wide spectrum of institutions, from junior colleges to universities with a major interest in research. Arrangements for their government must take account of the differences of function, and also of different local traditions. However, some general principles can be suggested:

1 Under the Council there will have to be a structure of committees, which will prepare major business and have delegated power on minor matters. The constitution of each committee depends on its business; for instance, the student welfare committee will have a substantial representation of students, while the committee concerned with the detailed supervision of the curriculum will need experts from the academic staff and also independent critical voices from outside. It is useful to start by laying out a structure for the committees, since the size of the Council depends on the number of chairmen of the various reporting committees who will need to be members.

2 Where there is an easily identifiable constituency (for example, all students, all technical staff) appointment should be by election with proportional representation and a secret ballot, though it may be necessary to enlighten the electorate about the work to be done and the qualities expected for its performance. Where the constituency is more vague (for example, employers of graduates, representatives of cultural interests) a two-stage system can be used, with a large and very widely representative annual meeting – like the Court of most English universities – which elects, by postal ballot, persons falling into certain defined classes.

3 The smallest body which has an appropriate balance and contains sufficient competence is to be preferred.

As an example of a possible structure for a *university* governing body, I offer the following:

The Pro-Chancellor *(lay chairman)*

The Vice-Chancellor *(chief executive)*

The Treasurer *(lay chairman of the Finance Committee)*

A senior administrative officer *(the choice depends on the structure of the organization)*

The Librarian

Six representatives of senior academic staff *(elected) (this provides for the senior representation of 'faculties')*

Four representatives of junior academic staff *(elected)*

Two representatives of administrative staff *(elected)*

Four representatives of other non-academic staff *(elected) (say, one each by secretaries, technicians, library staff and others)*

Four representatives of students *(elected)*

Nine representatives of general educational, research and cultural interests *(elected by those members of Court who represent such interests from outside the university)*

Five representatives of community interests *(elected by those members of the Court who represent such interests)*

Four representatives of employers and managements *(elected by those members of the Court who represent such interests)*

Three external co-opted members *(to provide for a possible need for specialists as chairmen of sub-committees)*

_____

Total Forty-six

A strict adherence to the principle of competence might shorten this list somewhat; but the range of duties to be covered has to be remembered. Thus, on an issue of safety at work the representative of the technicians might have the competence to make a contribution; while on an issue relating to the housing of students, and their integration with the surrounding community, the community representatives (some probably drawn from local government) could be helpful. A deliberate emphasis has been given to representation of educational, cultural and research interests, because it is here that people capable of intelligent comment on academic affairs would be most likely to appear.

The line of argument so far pursued can thus be used fairly easily to devise a new constitution for a university, which is an independent legal entity under its Charter or Act, but it is liable to conflct with the principle theoretically applied in the public sector and with voluntary (for example, church) colleges, where the owning body regards the college as a subsidiary to be governed by its nominees, even if they fail to cover more than a few of the legitimately interested parties and fail also to provide a sufficient range of competence. However, the principle just mentioned is not applied consistently: the freedom given in practice to the Academic Board detracts considerably from the influence of the owning authority; and there is a continuing discussion (which in 1978 surfaced in the deliberations of the Oakes Committee) about the limitation of local authority control. My position on this issue is that legal ownership ought not to bias the constitution of a governing body so that it becomes less competent. If colleges remain as the property of local authorities or of church or other voluntary bodies, it is sufficient that the owners should have an ultimate reserve power to close them down or to dismiss their governing bodies; in all normal circumstances, it is right to appoint the best possible Council and give it the fullest practicable autonomy to carry out the stated purposes. If owning authorities insist on meddling, and deny this autonomy, they will establish a case for making *all* colleges into independent legal entities like universities.

Thus far, then, I have argued for a single-headed or 'unitary' government, to be exercised by a balanced group chosen mainly for their evident competence to contribute to the decisions to be made, and allowed the greatest possible freedom to conduct affairs as they wish and, within their terms of reference, to make new experiments. But that freedom plainly cannot include the right of unlimited access to the public purse. How should the distribution of State finance for higher education be handled?

It will be seen from Chapter 1 that no tidy solution is immediately practicable, because higher education is mixed up with 'further education' at a level similar to or below that of sixth-form studies in the schools, and there are a number of different systems of financial control. In Chapter 5, I foresee a system which would contain junior or community colleges, teaching institutions not going beyond undergraduate courses, others going to the Masters' degree level, and others with major research interests and a potentiality for training doctoral candidates. This system would, as suggested on p. 47, continue to overlap with further education. However, the 'higher education' element of finance of further education can be segregated, and the Oakes committee report (p. 42) proposes new ways of managing it. It is therefore quite possible at any time, and certainly well before the year 2000, to have a single authority to distribute grants for every kind of higher education.

This solution has occasionally been proposed, but has met with opposition, and an alternative at one time suggested was to have a 'Polytechnic Grants Committee' parallel to the University Grants Committee; this would have left unanswered the questions about the sources of finance of non-polytechnic higher education colleges, junior colleges, and the remaining pure teacher training colleges. The reasons for having separate funding arrangements for universities appear to be concerned with the protection of their special status, and they do not appear to me to be strong, when set against the desirability of assisting the development of a rational division of functions by having a single body looking at finance. There are fears that the supposedly intimate relations achieved between the University Grants Committee and its wards would become impersonal and bureaucratic if a Grants Committee had a wider mandate. But the intimate relations are largely an illusion; the extent of personal contact between the University Grants Committee and universities is very small (much less, for instance, than that existing between HM Inspectors and the teacher training colleges), and the relations are essentially 'bureaucratic' in the sense of being based on (inadequate) paper records.

I therefore have no hesitation in supporting the view that there should be a single Higher Education Grants Committee, responsible for the distribution to all institutions concerned with higher education of central government funds. That committee should be more representative of the users of higher education and research, and less representative of the providers, than the present University Grants Committee; but the principle of using people to guide the system who are chosen for their knowledge and competence should remain. It should work through a regionally-based Inspectorate in constant personal touch with the universities and colleges being aided, and able to interpret their needs to the centre and to explain central policy to the recipient institutions.

There remain some important questions about the nature of these grants. If they are specific, tied to particular programmes or to a particular staff establishment, obedience to a master plan can be ensured, but the university or college will have an incentive to maximise its estimates for each separate programme, and no incentive at all to seek out economies and review priorities. If on the other hand the grant is a general or block allocation, the incentive to be ingenious in its application is provided at the cost of a possible departure from the purposes for which the funds were intended. If the income of the institution is mainly or entirely derived from a block grant, related to student numbers only in the sense that the granting authority has made its own forward estimates of those numbers, there will be no incentive to increase 'productivity' by taking more students; in fact, the incentive will run the other way, for a quieter life can be bought by having fewer students. If the grant includes an element which is related to *actual* student numbers, it will become to the Treasury an open-ended commitment, and no Government will be happy to approve it. If the income is derived in part from student fees, questions will arise about the ability of students to pay them.

There is no trick which will realise all the advantages and

obviate all the disadvantages; a compromise is necessary. This might in the year 2000 take the following form for those institutions which have a major commitment to higher education:

1   Each university or college would receive a block grant, forming part of a five-year rolling programme in which (save by express intervention of Parliament) the next two years are firm, the third year not expected to be altered by a large proportion, and the final two years provisional. Price changes would be dealt with by a method announced in advance. A system of this kind appears to be the right compromise between the desire for security in forward planning and the desire to allow adaptation to unexpected circumstances.

2   This would be tied to a specified range of purposes: that is, an institution would not be allowed to alter its main purposes without approval. A community college would be financed to provide two-year courses, but not degree courses. Other colleges would be recognized up to B.A. or up to M.A. level, as suggested in Chapter 5. But within the agreed purposes, there would be great freedom to experiment, as suggested in Chapter 4.

3   Capital and equipment expenditure would be financed by interest-bearing loan, the interest and repayment being a charge on the recurrent grant. This implies that each institution would be able to make proper economic choices between having crowded or old buildings, but more to spend on other things, and having new buildings and lavish equipment, but less to spend elsewhere. It could also make rational choices about labour-saving equipment. (The present separation of capital and current accounts means that the institutions have an incentive to put in extravagant claims for buildings and equipment, and these are kept in check only by a series of vexatious and wasteful controls, involving detailed approval of plans for buildings. Great savings of public money would have been achieved if this elementary economic point had been noted during the expansion period of the 1960s.)

4   The block grant would be supplemented by fees amount-

ing to at least twenty-five per cent of total income, exclusive of research grants. The availability of such fees is discussed below. The fee income would be available for any purpose within the agreed remit of the institution; its purpose would be to provide a constant reminder that costs should be adjusted to output, and that there is an advantage to be won by higher productivity.

5   In accordance with the proposals in Chapter 8, major research, as opposed to general scholarship, would be separately funded. This funding would be a mixture of specific grants for particular pieces of research, as at present, and more general block grants to departments chosen as being – for a period of years – substantial centres of research in a subject, which they could then use with reasonable freedom to follow lines of enquiry chosen by themselves. The purpose of allowing a selective and controlled freedom in this way is to secure obedience to a national policy of concentration of research and of doctoral work, while not confining research to items which appeal to a central committee or administrator.

The proposal to have substantial student fees is fully consistent with a better method of student finance. At present, British students accepted for a first degree course, not having previously accepted support for some other course, get their maintenance, subject to a means test, and their fees paid by local authorities, but, in effect, almost entirely by central government, which reimburses the cost. Students on shorter courses, and those repeating or adding to their studies at first degree level, can get 'discretionary' grants, but this gives rise to considerable variations in treatment. Higher degree students can get support if they have particular merit, but only up to a limit provided for their subject. The means test for first degree students is, for all younger students, related to their parents' means, even though they may have got well past the age at which they would, if not engaged in higher education, have expected to be independent of their parents. This dependence is a source of grievance, and also of much injustice and poverty caused by the failure of parents to meet their assessed contribution.

The British grant system is, by international standards,

generous: but it is generous to a chosen minority, who as a consequence of that generosity may reasonably expect to enjoy a substantially higher income for the rest of their life. It has therefore often been suggested that the costs should be met by loans, so that the beneficiaries of higher education ultimately meet its costs – and perhaps appreciate its value more fully because it is not handed to them free. There are successful loan systems in other countries, but also some identifiable disadvantages, particularly the danger that some people who particularly need encouragement to use educational opportunities will be put off by the prospect of incurring a debt.

But there is much to be said for a compromise arrangement. Under this, the cost of maintenance and fees would be available to any citizen for higher education courses, which he or she is qualified to enter, taken at any time of life, up to a maximum which initially might be two years. These grants would be free of parental means test, and fully transferable from one institution to another. Beyond this, loans subject to a very generous maximum would be available, with concessionary rates of interest and a flexible period of repayment, to cover maintenance and fees during the continuation of a course or for any additional courses which the student may wish to take – at any time of his life, and at any institution of higher education. These loans would become repayable when the earned income of the individual concerned, without regard to a husband's or wife's income, exceeded a certain minimum, set at a level which would be index-linked, so that there would be protection for those who fall on evil times, and no transfer of a wife's liability to her husband (such a transfer might discourage the higher education of women). By the end of the century there must surely be a consolidation of all financial transactions between the individual and the state, for both taxes and benefits, into a single computer-based system; loans and their repayment could be accommodated in such a system. It might be desirable to provide in addition for scholarships based on proven ability, covering a part of the costs, to act as an incentive to good performance in courses exceeding two years and to perform the functions at present carried out by studentships for higher degrees.

It is easy to invent ways in which such a system could be exploited. Some loans would never be repaid – they would have to be extinguished at retirement age or death. But, with a mixed system, the *size* of the loans would not be so intimidating as to provide a big incentive to evasion, and the experience of countries which have loans suggests that most people use the system fairly and honestly. The line between grants and loans could be varied – for instance, some day the state might provide full support for three years instead of two. Most of the problems about special cases would disappear; people would make their free choices about the duration and timing of higher education, but with a reminder that they are buying a probable benefit which should be paid for, and that they have no automatic right to a gift from the state to cover the full cost. Overseas students could be left to find their own fees and maintenance, from their own resources or from their governments, at the same rates as British students; but within the EEC an effort would be made to provide reciprocity – that is, to treat other EEC nationals as entitled to grant on the same basis as British students. Countries which do not levy fees often have systems of higher education which cost much more in student maintenance (and in loss of the opportunity of earnings), so it cannot rightly be concluded that, because some countries abolish fees, therefore we must do so also.

A likely result of a loans system would be to increase the demand for 'taught course' higher degrees (MAs and the equivalent) and other shorter courses, taken as an additional qualification in later life. This would help to adapt the skills of the community to changing circumstances. But it is by no means certain that loans would discourage those who desire further study purely for reasons of personal enrichment. There might be an increase in the numbers coming forward of these also; but, if this did not happen, the balance could be put right by providing supplementary scholarships in subjects which have a cultural rather than a vocational import-ance. The amount of any loan would be adjusted to cover family responsibilities.

The finance of higher education is, let me repeat, necessarily a compromise; but the systems proposed in this chapter are, I believe, a better compromise than we enjoy at present, providing the most essential freedoms while preserving an incentive to make sensible decisions and keeping the main shape of the system within a general social control.

10
WAY-OUT IDEAS — OR ARE THEY?

A number of readers of this book will by now feel a sense of disappointment that its discussion has been in terms of universities and colleges, courses and examinations, research units and facilities which, though altered, remain similar to those which already exist. Surely, they will say, the great movements of ideas and of technology will produce much more radical change in the next twenty years, and it will be of no use to cling to the methods and institutions of the past. I happen to believe that those who take a special interest in predicting our future state tend usually to overestimate the rate of change, by a large margin. Nevertheless there are many new ideas which deserve serious discussion, and some will certainly have a significant place by the year 2000, and an important influence on what happens after that.

The most radical of these belong to the disciples of Ivan Illich (*Deschooling Society*, Harper and Row, 1971). They see society as over-much dominated by institutions and professions which claim to be the means of achieving a particular end. Thus we have a Health Service which is in reality a Sickness Service, the emphasis being on curing already existing disease in accordance with the ideas or fashions currently held by the medical profession. So also learning, which should be the free choice of the individual, becomes something imposed on him by teaching institutions. The public is 'forced to support, through regressive taxation, a huge professional apparatus of educators and buildings which in fact restricts the public's chance for learning to the services the profession is willing to put on the market.'

Instead, Illich proposes the creation of 'learning webs' which would provide, for those who choose to use them, access to learning resources at any time. There would be no set curriculum, and no requirement to obtain a particular certificate of achievement. Libraries, laboratories and the like would exist for students to use at their own free will; there would be a system for putting people in touch with those who have skills to share or educational services to offer, or with those who might be partners in a particular learning venture.

To some writers, for example Paulo Freire, the whole existing learning system is a mirror of the oppressive nature of society: that is, the teacher decides and imposes the education, and the student must meekly accept what is offered. In a truly free education, the student and the teacher would learn together as they sought to solve real problems of human society. In this partnership, the teacher would offer a richer fund of knowledge and experience, but his conclusions would be reached only after considering what his students have to say. Taken to their limit, such ideas plainly involve a destruction of existing institutional arrangements, of a kind which Illich would welcome.

These discussions are not easy to relate to the process of learning how to find whether a particular mathematical series is convergent, or of learning why particular substances are poisonous to human beings. It is true that in the 'softer' areas of the social sciences and humanities, where there are few facts and many opinions, a teacher might be held 'oppressive' if he seeks to indoctrinate his students with a particular set of opinions without referring to equally plausible alternatives. But it is a ridiculous perversion to suppose that such teaching is typical of higher education in Britain or in most other countries. And we can rephrase the Illich contention by saying that learning is *organized* for the individual by teaching institutions, rather than being imposed on him; in higher education there is commonly a choice of courses of different kinds, and the choice to take none of them is always open. It is difficult to conceive that an advanced society could possibly work

without some degree of organization of a curriculu
testing of performance. Whatever doubts we may hav
instance, about the aims and methods of the medical profess
few of us would be happy to rely, in a medical emergency, \
those who had developed their skills entirely by their own
free choice from a catalogue of learning opportunities.

Nevertheless, we can take from the extremes of radical
thinking some important points. Although institutions are
necessary to education, they are not the whole of it, and perhaps
we do not provide sufficient informal opportunities of learning,
free from the restrictions of a set curriculum. I phrase this
with some caution, because we already have in Britain a
substantial informal education by radio and television (including the possibility of using Open University programmes), and
vast opportunities exist for anyone who makes full use of the
libraries provided in every area. It is not certain that the demand
for even more informal opportunities exists; but let us at least
be careful not to impose the restrictions of formal organization
unless they are necessary.

Institutional education very probably imposes on students too
rigid a framework for their learning. Lectures and seminars are
readily organized, and fit into a timetable; they can very easily
reduce the willingness to use less organized methods of learning,
such as broad reading in a library. It has long been noticed
that many students read nothing on their subject of study
unless it has been prescribed as a text. But a more important
issue is that raised on p. 31; students are very varied, and learn
best in different ways, yet institutions persist in treating them
as broadly homogeneous material, each to follow the same
timetable and to be prescribed the same work. It is not surprising that Illich's vision of freedom has a wide attraction.

The idea that groups of students should seek a curriculum
of their own choice is not a new one. The theory of the Workers
Educational Association is that the local branch, that is the
students, should decide what subjects are to be provided, and
the Association should then do its best to follow this decision.
In other words, the Association is organized from the students

upward, whereas the (much larger) adult education provision by the local authorities is organized from the top down. The distinction in real life is not so clear as this, and if one passes from unexamined adult courses to courses for specific qualifications, student choice is necessarily constrained by what the validating authority is prepared to approve. Nevertheless, there is room – especially in providing continuing education later in life – for a greater extent of adaptation to student choice than exists at present. It is not enough simply to provide some options at the margin, for the main aims and balance of the course may not be what is wanted. It would be good, for instance, to see a college giving notice in March of a higher degree course in the following October, applicants being invited to come to a preliminary meeting in June to work out with the staff concerned just how the time can best be used.

The idea that teachers should treat their students as partners in a search for knowledge, not as mere passive recipients of information and ideas, is also not new. The best of small-group teaching in Britain has embodied such a partnership. Nor is it necessary that the choice of subject for discussion should always be made by the teacher. Students ought to be encouraged to use the various types of teaching as a resource which, with private reading, will enable them to cover enough of the area to be examined, but they should not expect their teachers to dictate an all-sufficient text book to them. An excellent education can be found in going up the by-ways of students' own interests and concerns, and using this to illustrate the main principles of the course. What cannot be accepted from the radical approach is that students should decide the limits of discussion, requiring it, for instance, all to be set in a Marxist or Maoist framework. Teachers must have their freedoms too.

The desire for radical change in higher education has made more headway in other countries than in Britain, and in doing so has revealed some of the difficulties and contradictions which reformers too easily forget. The British system may accept, at the margin, some of the ideas for change, in the manner which I have indicated above, but this is not the way in which it will be transformed. However, a more subtle influence is exercised by two groups of people who do not question the main purposes and content of higher education as it now exists, but simply assert that it, or some large part of it, can be better provided in another way. One group is questioning the need for so much full-time higher education in separate universities and colleges, each devising its own curriculum; the other group sees the possibility of great changes from new educational technologies. These groups overlap, but it is convenient to discuss them separately.

The first group points to the success of the Open University, and to the low cost per graduating student it has achieved, and argues that it would be cost-effective to put resources into a great expansion of this type of part-time education. (Other types of part-time education do not generally have the same cost advantage, apart from relieving the Exchequer of the cost of student maintenance; so I discuss the case in relation to the Open University, where it is strongest.) It is important to be clear about what the Open University is, since in the public mind it tends to be mainly associated with its television and radio broadcasts. The essence of the Open University is a system of 'correspondence courses' backed by local tutors, and including the publication of special books, the provision of practical work kits, and an elaborate arrangement for criticizing and assessing written work. This central system is supplemented by television and radio courses, though it may well prove better to distribute many of these, not 'broadcast', but in cassette form. It is also supplemented by periods of intensive study at residential Summer Schools, for those able to attend.

In other words, the Open University uses an appropriately chosen variety of teaching technologies to provide instruction to part-time students. Its economy arises from providing the same course to a very large group of students; if it diversified its offerings so that it provided for small minorities, the economy would be much less evident. Since a course is used by so many students, it becomes possible and worth while to devote great care to its preparation, and to the choice of the best media to convey its message. Considering their careful preparation, Open University courses ought to be the finest in the land; in practice, this is often not the case, and this points to a problem in the recruitment of appropriate staff to this unusual institution, and also to a danger – that the faults and biases of a centrally controlled curriculum affect a large number of students, and, in the absence of any direct competitor, are not readily put right.

Although an Open University student may receive teaching similar in content to that which he would get in an ordinary university, it is evident that his educational experience is very different. He (or she) does not have the informal influences of constant association with fellow students, and his personal contact with teachers is much less. Even more than in the rest of higher education, he is subjected to a uniform process. On the other hand, his motivation is more fully tested, for he must give up much of his spare time for several years to arduous private study; and because, in most cases, the student will be at work, or looking after a home and children, the opportunities of cross-fertilization with the experiences of everyday life will be greater than with those whose study is full-time.

If one asks whether a greater proportion of higher education should be provided in this way, the answer must evidently depend on the replies to two further questions. First, is this different and part-time educational experience a proper substitute for full-time study, or should it be reserved for those who have missed opportunities of full-time study earlier in life or who have shown themselves late developers? Second, even if a larger provision for part-time education existed (whether through the Open University or by courses in local colleges) would there be enough people with the time and the persistence to make proper use of it? There is no ready answer to the first of these questions, but an attempt can be made on these lines. Full-time higher education provides both the initial requirements of certain jobs, and a maturing process for those who will occupy positions of responsibility in society. There is no possibility of abolishing it altogether; but, if it is reduced, which students are to be diverted to the part-time mode, which normally will imply taking a job not requiring higher education, and postponing for some years the attainment of an equivalent qualification? The condition for such a diversion is evidently that full-time higher education is over-producing in relation to the immediate economic needs of society (which may well be true; see p. 23), and the appropriate nature of the diversion would be the weaker students of non-vocational subjects – that is, those who have no immediate need to obtain a degree or other qualification, and who can appropriately be challenged to prove their motivation by using the part-time route. But then the second question becomes relevant. Such students would be rather likely to lack the necessary persistence. The most powerful motive to engage in part-time study arises when a vocation which has had a large non-graduate entry offers extra rewards to graduates. School teaching has been much the largest example of this, but before long there will be no recent non-graduate entrants to that profession, and it is not at all certain that groups of qualification-hunters of comparable size will appear elsewhere. It may well be, then, that by the year 2000 interest in arduous courses of part-time study will be found mainly among a diminishing group of those who missed earlier opportunities, and a (hopefully increasing) group of those who want to obtain new or additional qualifications, or simply to broaden their minds by new types of study, whatever their previous education.

There may be justification here for some increase in the Open University type of provision, or, more accurately, in the total provision made for part-time study, but not for a significant *diversion* from full-time study. If government thinks that too much money is being spent on indifferent sociologists or English students, it can try to reduce the provision for them directly, though with evident problems in persuading autonomous institutions to do what is wanted. There is no need then to pay for equivalent alternative part-time places, for most of them would never be used. The Open University offers very important possibilities in the continuing education of adults, and it should be financed for those types of course, not necessarily at degree level, where a sufficiently large group of strongly motivated students can be found. It does not provide a sensible alternative to existing universities and colleges in initial higher education.

The revolution which is foreseen by the educational technologists is not easily described, for the focus of interest has shifted. In the 1960s and 1970s there was much interest in 'audio-visual aids', and in particular in the teaching uses of television, which are particularly well established in medicine but could, it was thought, be widely used elsewhere. The experience of this period was, however, disappointing, for two reasons. First, the enthusiasts had over-estimated the acceptability of television-based courses; disturbing evidence began to be cited that students not only prefer the immediate communication of a human teacher, but may actually learn more from rather indifferent personal teaching than they do from a more polished television presentation. However, the facts on this are not clear, and there remained, of course, the presentation which television alone could give – for instance, a close-up view of an experiment provided simultaneously to hundreds of students. More seriously, however, the economics of the matter had not been rightly judged. A television based course, or a multi-media course, using, for instance, films or film strip and sound recordings, requires a very considerable investment in its preparation. This is worth while for the Open University, though some even of its programmes are lacking in polish; the number of potential students justifies the investment. But most higher education institutions set a high importance on the special features of their courses; they do not find it readily possible even to incorporate sections from Open University courses. It is not worth while to make a proper job of a television-based course which will be used by, perhaps, a hundred students a year for two or three years, until it is superseded or requires alteration, and which has little chance of significant sales elsewhere. Institutions found themselves being asked for large appropriations of money for media services, with no apparent savings elsewhere, and no strong general feeling that a better teaching job would follow if the money were spent. The result has been to deflate the brave expectations, and to concentrate attention on the special uses, like demonstration experiments, where a point can be made much more quickly and forcibly by the use of television or other media aids.

But a more far-reaching change in technology is now potentially available. Its enthusiasts see the home or study room of the future as equipped with a visual display unit and as having access to a high speed printer. The visual display unit will incidentally receive broadcast television programmes, and its associated sound unit will receive broadcast radio. It will receive from the broadcast channels a wide range of information services, such as are provided by the Ceefax and Oracle services of the BBC and ITV. It will also be linked by cable (which could serve additionally to carry telephone calls) to data banks of virtually limitless extent. Whole books could be called up for viewing, or, if they are needed for reference, printed out on the printer – which is also envisaged as distributing the daily newspaper.

Thus far the vision is rather like having instant access to the British Library or the Library of Congress, and the enthusiasts may need to be reminded that you can only call up information if you know what you want. For the purpose of suggesting ideas and indicating leads to be followed, the very old-fashioned technology of a bookcase full of relevant printed books will continue to have many advantages. But there is more to come. The data bank can be seen as a superior version of the fallible memory of a teacher. Between it and the student can be placed the technology needed to provide the equivalent of a dialogue with a teacher. The student can be taken, by programmed learning techniques, through the steps of an argument, his errors being corrected and the right path being implanted in his memory. Computer-based learning of this kind has of course been the subject of experiment for some time, but now it has become possible for sophisticated learning processes to be handled by microprocessors or low-cost mini-computers. The possibility that it may be economically worth while to displace the human teacher begins to look like a real one.

Again, the enthusiasts need several reminders. Programmed learning has an evident application to the acquiring of a set of techniques – for instance, in the differential and integral calculus. It has to be approached with more care if the student's interest is, say, to acquire a critical appreciation of the plays of Ibsen. A first-level programme, teaching a series of parrot-like responses, plainly will not do – it would rightly be open to the charge of indoctrination. A higher level programme, seeking to help the student to ask the right questions without dictating answers on matters which are properly ruled by emotional response or personal taste, would be conceivable – but can one with assurance even set out the right questions? Perhaps the programme has to be about learning to ask the right questions, or about learning how to learn to ask them . . . and so on, in infinite recess. The problem here is the extreme difficulty of defining just what the learning process is, once one leaves the safe ground of ascertained facts and set methods.

There are also some very grave practical difficulties. The number of separate bits of the learning process – for all kinds of course in all institutions – is immense. Each displacement of the human teacher, in a single element of learning, will require the development of 'software' – that is, the set of instructions to the mini-computer for its side of the dialogue. It may require several different versions of the software, if the 'hardware' is not standardized. Software development is complex and expensive, and a considerable volume of use will be needed to justify it. This suggests dangers of centralization – as if there were only one textbook on a subject – or, if competing sources exist, very great difficulty in getting a sufficient range of commercially viable packages. Furthermore, the new technology would have to make its way, not only against the Luddite attitudes of those who may lose their jobs, but against the more subtle arguments of particular teaching institutions that the packages on offer do not quite fit the programme of teaching which they think best.

This technical revolution, therefore, looks like falling a long way short of a major displacement of traditional methods, at least in the next twenty years. In consequence, it will not displace traditional institutions; the vision of a student who never has to stir from his bedroom at home need not trouble us at this time. Two developments do, however, seem likely by the year 2000. One is the wide availability of cheap programmable units which can assist learning in the areas where knowledge of facts or of precisely defined methods are important, and of a range of modular software packages in some at least of those areas. The other is the supplementation of library resources by easy access to very large data banks; though this will be more significant for the researcher than for most higher education students (for whom the old-fashioned book will usually remain adequate, relatively cheap and convenient).

But if existing higher education is neither to be 'deschooled', nor transformed into a giant Open University, nor wholly revolutionized by the silicon chip, ought we to look for the signs of other major changes? One of these, in the British context, might be the appearance of more courses in which the qualification is obtained by obtaining credit in a series of separate modules. If such a pattern became general, the further step might be taken of allowing the credits to be accumulated at different institutions, and not necessarily over a consecutive period of time. The problems of allowing student mobility would be solved at a stroke, and the opportunity of testing higher education would be opened up to people who could only afford the time or money to take one or two modules. Interrupting a course for personal reasons would no longer carry serious disadvantages, since the credits obtained would be available to be used at a later date.

But, attractive as these possibilities are, such a development is neither likely nor desirable, except perhaps for an extension of facilities to take single modules not leading to a qualification.

It is not likely because British higher education courses are relatively short, and they tend to be planned as a whole or in two parts, with a close relation between the courses in a particular subject. The degree of separation implied in a modular structure with an option to the student to go away in the middle is really not possible. (See p. 71.) The development is not desirable because it implies substantial central control of the curriculum, which would have at each institution to be divided into the same number of parts, with some arrangement for providing a reasonable match between the parts wherever they were studied. This would involve a serious loss of the freedom to experiment with new patterns of course.

I have already given, in Chapter 7, my reasons for believing that examinations will continue, though they should be both reformed and kept in their place. Indeed, if there was a serious attempt to abolish qualifications obtained by examination, the result would be the appearance of a new set of examinations controlled by employers, which would be subject to more faults than the assessment they had displaced. The happy student dream, of learning for learning's sake free from any anxiety about the assessment of results, is therefore likely to remain a dream. Nor is there much likelihood of parts of higher education becoming student-controlled (a development for which there are venerable precedents), for students do not pay the bills, and the state, which pays most of them, is most unlikely to regard the consumers of the product as ideal governors. Students will have to be prepared to remain as partners with several other interests in the government of their institutions.

There are, however, two developments, once considered 'way out', which may begin to have reality. One may seem an administrative detail, but it has a wider significance: it is time for higher education to free itself from the restrictions of a pattern of three terms, divided by lengthy vacations. This is a survival from a past age, which has lingered because it is highly convenient to members of the academic staff. But there is no reason whatever to think that thirty weeks (or sometimes less) out of fifty-two is an optimum period of study for students;

in modern conditions, the idea that they engage in extensive private study in vacations is fanciful. The effect of having a limited period for study is to reduce the amount which can be covered, or to increase to a dangerous extent the stress during the weeks of term; but also to remove from the system some of the flexibility which it might offer to students, to repeat courses or to pursue additional options or simply to go rather more slowly over a part of the ground.

I must emphasize that I am not proposing the continuous use of buildings and equipment by means of a 'Box and Cox' arrangement, in which different students are present at different times, thus giving a larger flow through the system. Schemes for this, involving a six-term year, have been drawn up and costed; in a period of rapid expansion, such as the 1960s, they would have given large capital savings, but no significant reduction in current cost. But the requirements for the rest of the century do not involve a lot of extra student places, so there is no point in suffering the undoubted social disadvantages of such a system. My proposal is that the normal student year should be around forty weeks, which would leave four weeks for family holidays, and eight for other purposes such as travel; that the extra time should be used, in part to reduce the intensity of courses, and make it reasonable to resist demands to add an extra year, and in part to provide supplementary opportunities of study so that courses can be improved and failures reduced.

This change would apparently involve some cost for additional academic staff, if opportunities for scholarship and research are to be maintained; but if, as seems likely in the 1990s (see p. 139) student numbers are falling, the 'cost' may be no more than making a better use of the staff already there. The cost to the state for student maintenance would not be very great: first, because very substantial sums are claimed by students in supplementary benefit during vacations, and this could cease, grants being related to the full calendar year; and, second, because for students living away from home in halls of residence the cost per week for an extra ten weeks would generally be less than the cost for the first thirty. Universities and colleges would complain about losing conference trade (though this in fact seldom occupies a high proportion of the vacant beds); but academic conferences could be accommodated in the remaining twelve weeks of the year, and there would be no great disadvantage in losing the general conference and holiday letting trade, which is a doubtful diversion of educational energies.

I hope at least to see some loosening of the pattern of the academic year, and I believe that the common-sense of this may be recognized. The other possible development is towards freer access. Most higher education courses in Britain are selective, and entry is competitive. Even the open doors of the Open University are closed when the year's quota of students has been accepted. There is no school examination which guarantees entrance to higher education, and the schools justifiably complain of the stress among those who are trying to ensure success in getting to the institution of their choice. Universities and colleges maintain elaborate and time-consuming systems for getting the right number of entrants, and for attracting to their own particular doors those of the best quality; and yet the gap between the number of plausibly qualified candidates and the number of admissions is commonly quite small, so the effect of all the machinery of admission is, taking all institutions together, of little consequence.

There is no good reason, in my view, why a right to enter some sort of higher education should not be conferred by a level of performance equivalent to holding two Advanced level passes in the present General Certificate of Education. That right would be an obvious one to offer if, as suggested in Chapter 5, colleges with two-year courses are developed. There cannot be an unrestricted right to enter a course in a particular subject (say, medicine), or at a particular place, for the facilities available cannot be suddenly changed to provide for an influx of students, and some subjects have a provision determined by the needs of the labour market. But a simpler, two-stage system of admission would become possible. In the first stage, candidates would get *advice* from the institutions they wish to consider, and would ask questions about what is offered. At this stage, some would be given firm offers, and some would be warned of a danger of failure if they proceed further. At the end of this stage, institutions would make a return of the number of places still available in each course, and candidates who have not accepted a place or dropped out would be invited to indicate, in order, a sufficient range of alternative preferences. At the second stage, those candidates still seeking a place who have the minimum qualification would be made an offer by a central registry, that offer conforming as nearly as possible to their preferences. The higher education institutions would have an incentive to make as many firm offers as possible in Stage 1 (for the Stage 2 candidates would be directed to them by an outside office); but the elaborate arrangements for perceiving minute distinctions of quality among mediocre candidates would not be necessary. There would be less worry, and a few candidates, at present excluded, who – though warned of their weakness – decide to try their luck, would be sure of a place. Such a system could be supplemented by allowing mature students without the formal minimum qualification to attempt courses in two-year colleges if they wish to do so, and (if successful) to go on to further study elsewhere. Such students would be self-selected by the strength of their motivation, and the risks of waste in an open entry of this kind are probably quite small.

There is, of course, a much more revolutionary version of the doctrine of open entry, namely that higher education should be (like school education) a right of every citizen. But it is very difficult to attach a meaning to this claim. If 'higher education' is defined (as in the Prologue to this book) as requiring a particular level of previous preparation, then it cannot effectively be a right of every citizen, for some will not have reached that level. If higher education is defined so that it is attainable by anybody, it becomes in effect the whole of adult education at all levels, a collection so heterogeneous as to be difficult to discuss in any sensible manner. Some may hold that higher education, in the proper sense, should be available to anyone who cares to try it, entirely at the choice of the individual and without regard to any previous qualification. Such openness of entry does indeed seem to be close to the practice in some countries, but there are two consequences. One is an erosion of standards, as attempts are made to avoid a cruel disappointment of students too weak to reach a proper level. The other is a drain on the public purse, to provide for some students who will never complete a course, and for others who take an unconscionable time doing so. The benefits of such a use of public money do not appear likely to be great, and certainly, in the British context, there are many better causes to which the taxpayer's money might be devoted.

11

1980-2000: WHAT COULD HAPPEN

I have suggested in the preceding chapters a number of changes in the structures and practices of British higher education which seem to me desirable during the remainder of this century. But, while some of these changes are likely to happen under the pressure of events, most of the important ones will need a constructive reforming zeal to bring them about. The existence of that zeal cannot be assured, and indeed a plausible interpretation of events and trends leads to a much less satisfactory forecast of what may happen.

Let us look back to the early 1960s. British higher education was growing fast, but statistics could be deployed showing it to be far behind that of the United States, which was then seen as the front-runner among nations in economic and technological matters. An advanced economy was believed to require very large numbers of highly educated people, and, since no one had thought very hard about this requirement, it was supposed that an expansion biased towards science and technology, but still of substantial extent in the humanities and social sciences, could be fully justified. Brave assumptions were made about the arrival of a 'new industrial revolution' in which high technology would produce rapid economic growth, and would thereby yield the resources to pay for more education: indeed, the prevailing view was that an investment in higher education was likely to be highly profitable to the nation as well as to each individual receiving the benefit. The expansion was popular with those of progressive sympathies, because it was seen as extending to able children from 'lower' social classes a privilege which had long existed for the wealthy and the professional classes. Students did not excite any particular antipathy among the public – indeed, why should they, since they were about to confer on all of us the benefits of greater riches earned through successful industrial and commercial change? No doubt they would, some of them, hold revolutionary ideas on the extremes of Left or Right, but so had some students in every previous generation, and it was well to get this nonsense out of the system when young; they would settle down to be reliable supporters of the Establishment when they had a wife and children to support.

A caricature, perhaps: but recognizable as the attitude of complacency and self-congratulation with which the members of the academic community embarked on a period of great expansion. They were honoured and essential claimants on the taxpayer's bounty. But it was not long before the unfolding of events destroyed the complacent assumptions. Three elements of that change can be distinguished. The first was produced by student unrest. The veterans of student conflict in this country must own to a sense of being mere minor members of a Fourth Division when they hear of the massive insurrections which, like some sudden infection, spread across the universities and colleges of other countries. Very little happened in Britain: no governments were rocked, no memorable martyrs were created, no significant concessions were made. But whereas the French student revolts appeared to have a clear political mission, and those in the United States could claim a moral purpose of protest against the Vietnam war, the sporadic troubles in Britain seemed to be created for trouble's own sake. The excuses for student occupations were flimsy, and in some instances wholly fabricated: the methods of agitation used involved false propaganda and deceit. The result was that the British public took a marked dislike to students, and began to be extremely critical of the institutions which failed to 'discipline' them, or did not even try. But in fact the older forms of disciplinary action, intended to deal with individual students most of whom were minors, were quite incapable of controlling mass movements composed of people who now reached the age of majority at eighteen. So various forms of recourse to the law had to be tried, and they revealed what an ineffective instrument the law could be.

A simple version of the gut feeling of the public about students was that, if they had all this time to make trouble, they could not be doing anything very useful. This developed into a more serious criticism, which is the second element of the change. People were no longer willing to accept that more higher education was a good thing, regardless of its content. More scientists and technologists might be a good thing, but the universities and colleges could not fill enough places in these practical subjects, and even in science and technology employers were making critical remarks about the quality of the students they were recruiting. But did we really need all these sociologists? Sociology became the great example of a subject in which the public had no confidence: provision for it had been expanded too fast, too many of the teachers appeared lightweight and too many of one political persuasion, and the students were foremost in finding time for disruption. But there were doubts about other subjects. The effectiveness of the economy appeared to be inversely related to the number of economists who studied its workings. Language departments did not seem to be producing people who could assist our understanding of the contemporary world. Schools of art encouraged the production of art-forms which many ordinary people found comic rather than inspiring. It will readily be seen that in such attitudes there was a failure to recognize wider educational purposes, and a too ready acceptance of usefulness and conventionality as the tests to be applied to higher education. But the important thing was that questions about purpose and use were being asked.

The third change was the consequence of the economic ill-success of Britain, and of the new economic policies which she (like other countries) felt bound to pursue in the difficult circumstances of the 1970s: restrictions of government expenditure, more careful budgetary control, high interest rates and the like. In earlier years new forms of welfare expenditure had been loaded on to the budget in response to public demands and political pressures, with little consideration for the ability of the economy to bear them. Now the pendulum swung the other way, and people began to think, not only of the absolute need for a particular kind of expenditure, but also of the relative importance it should be given within the total social budget. Higher education did not actually do too badly in this era of questioning and control, but there has been a considerable disappointment of previous inflated expectations, and a shock to morale when plans have been cut or when reasonable proposals for development have been frustrated.

One reason for the disappointment of expectations was the failure of students to come forward in the numbers which had been written into the forward estimates. This hiccup in student demand appears to have occurred in many countries, and may have been due to the effect on young people themselves, rather than their parents, of the period of student disruption and the increasing tendency to question the content and priority of higher education. But in Britain it could equally have been a straight economic effect. For a period in the 1970s, there was much talk of graduate unemployment, and there was obviously little incentive to put off the time when one would earn a normal income in order to take a course which might lead to having no earnings at all. (However, by the time of writing this book the labour market has greatly changed, and it is now broadly true that each extra increment of education improves the chances of employment, at least up to first degree level. Since it takes time for the understanding of this to reach those in the schools, it is too soon to know if this will cause an increase in student demand).

For some time it was possible to suppose that an upturn of economic fortunes would put higher education back on its path of expansion for many years to come; though the more numerate were aware that an expansion like that of the 1960s could not possibly continue long without producing far too large a diversion of the manpower and finances of the country.

But indefinite expansion, even if at a slower rate, solves so many problems – and surely it was needed, when we were so far behind the United States? However, this was to reckon without the effects of demography. The British birth rate rose to a peak just after the Second World War (no doubt because families were making good the deferment of births while men were away in the Forces), declined to a trough in the early 1950s, and then rose to a further peak in the early 1960s. From 1964 onwards, however, the birth rate fell heavily, though apparently bottoming out around 1978. This fall was partly related to a postponement of marriage and child-bearing, and a smaller average size of family; it was accelerated in the early 1970s because there were fewer young parents available to have families, as a consequence of the birth rate fall twenty years or so earlier.

The record of success in predicting birth-rates is not good, but it seems rather likely that numbers of births will rise through the 1980s, and then fall again. This is because some of the social factors which caused the decline in fertility may largely have completed their influence: indeed, if the age of beginning to have children is no longer rising, there will be a contribution to births as the deferred families are brought up to their intended size. At the same time, the number of potential parents will be greatly increased as a consequence of the 'baby boom' of the 1960s. It would take a massive further decline in fertility (no reason for which can at present be foreseen) to offset this increase in numbers of young potential parents.

Some of the consequences of these demographic fluctuations for higher education are set out in the Department of Education and Science 'Brown Paper', or discussion document, called 'Higher Education into the 1990s', which was issued in February 1978. This shows, on the middle of three projections, the total (full-time and sandwich course) student numbers in Great Britain rising from 504,700 in 1975/6 to 603,500 in 1985/6, and then falling slowly to 599,200 in 1989/90 and, much faster, to 519,500 in 1995/6. These figures already assume a significant increase in the proportions of each generation entering higher education. The turning-points for total student numbers are roughly two years after those for entrants; so, since the numbers of eighteen-year-old men and women seem likely to increase from 1997 or 1998 onwards, there should be a further turning-point of student numbers in or before the year 2000, though this is a possibility which (rather misleadingly) is not mentioned in the Brown Paper. The general position in each decade is:

1980s	*A modest hump in numbers*
1990s	*A catastrophic fall*
2000–2010	*(Probably) A partial recovery.*

The assumptions of the Brown Paper can be altered, for instance, by opening the gates of higher education more widely – as would be done if my recommendation about junior colleges was carried out. It is not credible, however, that such alterations could convert the fall of the 1990s into a rise. To do this, it would be necessary virtually to double the present 'age participation rates' – a feat which was admittedly performed between 1960 and 1971, but which would be more difficult to achieve a second time, and would (in the context of the changed public attitudes mentioned above) be most unlikely to get priority for financial support. The Brown Paper set out a number of alternative ways of tackling the situation: expanding the system in the 1980s and contracting it in the 1990s in line with student numbers; 'tunnelling through the hump' that is, underproviding places in the 1980s in order to avoid so much contraction later; providing places for the extra students without a corresponding increase in resources (and then, presumably, returning to the former standards in the 1990s); reducing the effective student load in the 1980s by recourse to two-year courses, part-time courses or deferment of entry; and seeking to increase demand in the 1990s, for instance by getting more students who are children of manual workers and by encouraging 'recurrent' (post-experience) education. But it is likely that no neat policy decisions will be taken in accordance with these alternatives. A more likely 'scenario' is as follows.

Up to about 1983 there will be little provision for extra student numbers, government hoping that the underprovision will be unnoticed or politically tolerable, or that it may even not appear at all if the institutions squeeze in bigger numbers without extra resources – which can be explained as a virtuous process of improving productivity. The Public Expenditure White Paper published in January 1979 (Cmnd. 7439) shows current expenditure per student in universities falling slightly up to 1980–81, and current expenditure per full-time-equivalent student in higher *and further* education falling slightly up to 1982–83. This, however, is a projection now discovered to be vulnerable to renewed expenditure cuts caused by efforts to control inflation. From 1982 to about 1988 the resources available will be held constant (the remaining hump being small enough to be a ready candidate for 'tunnelling'); and from 1988 onwards, and particularly after 1990, resources available will be allowed to decline, but probably more slowly than student numbers, the rate being determined by what can conveniently be achieved by natural wastage. (A high proportion of higher education expenditure is on salaries, and contracts and legislation give to most of the staff a great amount of security of tenure; so it is very difficult to reduce expenditure quickly. Indeed, a rapid run-down of staff would produce a peak of expenditure, because it would be necessary to buy out rights of tenure and meet large redundancy payments. The security of tenure provided is grossly excessive, but it has to be accepted, for staff now in post, as a fact of life.)

Rather more optimistic versions of this scenario are possible, if a resolute policy of opening up new opportunities, particularly in two-year colleges, is pursued. But Britain's fundamental economic problems not only continue, but grow deeper. I think that it remains likely, therefore, that the 1980s will be a decade of parsimony and the 1990s one of contraction – though with the distant prospect of some recovery beyond the year 2000. But the age-distribution of teaching staff in higher education is strongly skewed towards the younger end. This fact is illustrated, in the Brown Paper, for universities: the majority of staff in 1975 were under 40, and only ten per cent were over 55. It is believed that a similar distribution exists in the public sector colleges, as is indeed likely in any service which has recently had a major expansion. This implies that there will be relatively very few openings for replacing staff on retirement in the 1980s, and the rather larger number of retirements in the 1990s will (on the assumptions made above) provide an opportunity to reduce the resources available rather than to fill new posts. Only beyond 2000 A.D. can one see a likelihood of substantial freeing of posts by retirement, co-inciding with an expansion of student numbers, so that there could well be a crisis of recruitment at that period. A further implication of the skewed age distribution is that, for many years to come, there will be an acute 'promotion blockage' and consequent bad effects on morale.

It is sometimes supposed that the academic staff in higher education begin their working life full of new ideas, and then become gradually more conservative and set in their ways as they grow older. This does not conform with my experience. A majority, I think, always have rather limited and inflexible ideas, while an influential minority continue to have a fresh and innovative outlook. That minority, however, cannot rely on achieving innovation solely by exploiting the indolence of their more conservative colleagues; very often they achieve it only in the context of expansion, which enables the innovators to argue 'Let us try this out as an additional activity: none of your traditional activities need to be reduced or disturbed'. The prospect for the 1980s and 1990s is for an ageing staff, hardly refreshed at all by new recruitment, resentful of the pressures to economize and contract, and conscious that any significant new innovation can only be achieved by running down something which already exists.

This is a situation in which the conservative defence of established positions – whether those positions be good or bad – is likely to be tenacious and successful. The shift to a greater conservatism is indeed already apparent, both in universities and in public sector colleges; there is much less sense of exciting innovation than there was in the 1960s. (The word 'conservative' here implies a desire to preserve things, even if they ought to be changed, the opposite of 'radical', which implies a willingness to react to new situations by proposing new solutions. There is no suggestion of a relation to the Conservative Party, which is currently more radical than the Labour Party.) However, the higher education system is not well adapted even to the world of 1980, and the earlier pages of this book contain many suggestions for the changes needed by the year 2000. Therefore the reaction of the general public to academic conservatism is likely to be impatient; in consequence, it will become harder than ever to obtain resources for higher education; and an even greater stringency will strengthen the conservative tendencies.

I see little prospect, therefore, of a renewal of confidence and good relations between the public and the higher education institutions, even though the memories of student unrest are now fading. In my years of service on the Committee of Vice-Chancellors and Principals of the universities, there was a clear and increasing tendency for the majority to react to any external suggestion for change by a bland demonstration that nothing could sensibly be done, and to react also to the minority from more innovative universities by urging them not to 'rock the boat' and by excluding them from sensitive areas of the Committee's work. There was also in recent years a noticeable tendency not to appoint radicals as Vice-Chancellors, so that the conservative majority was increasing. In contacts with the polytechnics and other public sector colleges, I have noted their extreme defensiveness and urge towards self-justification. I would judge that they also have an increasing tendency to cold-shoulder their innovators. The teacher training colleges have had a particularly difficult problem of adapting after major surgery on their numbers, so it would be ungenerous to expect too much in the way of new ideas; but in most of the cases known to me, the range of innovation which they have considered is narrow and conventional. The picture of conservatism is confirmed on looking at particular subject areas: for instance, the reaction of most mathematicians to the manifest problems of mathematical education has been both conventional and unsuccessful.

These are tendencies which, on the arguments developed above, will get much worse. Can anything be done about this extremely depressing prospect? It is no sufficient answer to propose that radical innovations should be imposed by central decree. That is an ultimate possibility, if there is an extremely serious mismatch between public need and the practice of the institutions, but a uniform imposed change is not really a sign of life. What we want is a variety of spontaneous radical responses to new circumstances.

We must seek, therefore, means of strengthening the position of individual innovators within the higher education institutions. Changes in government, so as to bring academic as well as financial decisions under the scrutiny of well-informed people from outside, would help. What is lacking is enough people to ask awkward questions: 'Here is a new educational need – what are you doing about it? Why do you continue to do things in that way? How do you justify this distribution of your resources?' But there would be very powerful conservative opposition to any changes in forms of constitution which would make good this deficiency. Strong direction by government would be needed, to impose the changes.

Is it possible to assist innovation by increasing the opportunities for new recruitment? Some help would be given by increasing the number of early retirements of academic staff, and the net cost of this (bearing in mind that they would often be replaced at a lower salary level) might not be very great, and could be justified as an investment in flexibility, even during the next few years when the total number of academic staff may not change greatly. An alternative way of increasing flexibility would be to forbid the granting of any rights of tenure to newly appointed academic staff beyond those provided by the general law (which are quite adequate to protect freedom of expression). This is a step which ought to be taken, but it would be an exceedingly difficult one, with implications for other groups supported from the public purse; and, given the skewed age-distribution of staff, it would have little effect in the present century.

It is possible to do something to stimulate innovation by earmarking funds to support it, and this has been an occasional tactic of the University Grants Committee, even though it conflicts with the principle of making block grants which the recipient can spend as he wishes. There is a limit to the effectiveness of the method – those at the centre may not be able to make a good judgement about the right way to innovate, and indeed on occasion they have simply pointed to an apparent national need and left it to others to think of how to deal with it. Nevertheless, it may be desirable to extend the use, by the proposed Higher Education Grants Committee, of earmarked funds, to ensure that important new developments are not frustrated by the jealousy of those using funds for less urgent purposes.

However, such developments will only be identified, and their importance confirmed, if there is a continuing public discussion of higher education, its purposes, structure and methods. That discussion cannot safely be left to the academics, who are interested parties with established positions within existing structures and professional groups. It must involve a wider public with a concern for the products of higher education and for its place within the total social provision. My hope in writing this book has been to make a small contribution in stimulating the wider discussion, and thus releasing constructive reforming zeal.

INDEX

Aberdeen University, 38
academic year, 130–2
accountancy, 8, 20, 76, 77
administrative studies, 9
adult education, vii, 9, 71
Advanced Further Education Councils, 11, 42
agriculture, 4, 9
architecture, 9, 25
art, 24, 25, 78, 95; colleges, 3, 4, 14, 137
arts, 73, 101; fine, 68, 101; science v, 65–6
audio-visual aids, 126

Bar, the, 8
Bible, 25
biology, 76
birth rate, 30, 139
books, 63
British Academy, 106
British Library, 127
Business Education Councils, 7
business schools, 3
business studies, 9, 95

Cambridge University, 51; appraised, 57–9; control of, 104; degrees, 6; endowment income, 11, 57; Tripos exams, 61, 83–4
Carnegie Commission, viii, ix, 26, 49, 60; purposes defined in, 32
Carnegie Council, viii, 49–51, 60
Carnegie Foundation, 60
Ceefax, 127
'Central institutions', 2, 4
certificates, 6–7, 9
charitable status, 2
Charlotte Mason College, 14
Chaucer, 78
chemistry, 20
Chicago University, 62
churches, 2
classes, size of, 19
classes, social, bias towards 'upper', 58; educational attainment and, 30–1, 58
colleges, ix; numbers of, 3–4; tertiary, 55
Committee of Vice-Chancellors and Principals, 143
community colleges, 47–8, 49

comprehensive schools, 39
continuous assessment, 86–7
correspondence courses, 1, 123
Council for National Academic Awards, 7, 8, 11, 41, 104
craftsmanship, 68
Cranfield Institute of Technology, 2
credits system, 129–30
Cross, Patricia, 67, 68, 70
curriculum, 60–82, 120, 121; breadth v. depth, 63–5, 71, 78; content of, 63–4, 66–70; higher degrees in, 74; student choice of, 71–2, 121–2; subjects, 75–8; U.S. undergraduate, 60; for year 2000, 70, 78, 82

degree, university, attainment level, non-uniformity of, 14–15; 'classifying', 87; doctor's, 6, 18, 19, 20, 36, 51, 96, 112; in education, 9; external, 7; fees, 6, 16; first, 5, 6, 16, 51, 56, 71, 115; higher, 5, 6, 8, 16, 72, 115; institutions conferring, 2, 5, 6, 8; level, uniformity of, 49; master's, 6, 36, 51, 52, 56, 72, 112, 117; meaning of, ix; part-time, 36; research, 72–3; science v. humanities, 85; students ill-qualified for, 47–8; 'validation' of, 7; vocational intention and, 20
dentistry, 9
Department of Education and Science, 2
design colleges, 3, 4
Diploma of Higher Education, 46
diplomas, 6–7
direct grant institutions, 2, 3, 9, 11
drama, 68, 95; colleges, 3, 4
Durham University, 57

economics, 76, 77
Edinburgh University, 58
education, age of compulsory, vii; colleges of, 5, 6, 7, 8, 9, 14; the economy and, 21–4; 'post-compulsory', vii
EEC, 117
Emerson, R. W., 56
employers, 106; in educational government, 107, 108, 109, 110; examinations valuable to, 87–8; research and, 72–3; training by, vii, 23, 63, 71